First World War
and Army of Occupation
War Diary
France, Belgium and Germany

56 DIVISION
Divisional Troops
512 Field Company Royal Engineers
4 February 1916 - 30 April 1919

WO95/2942/2

The Naval & Military Press Ltd
www.nmarchive.com
Published in association with The National Archives

Published by

The Naval & Military Press Ltd

Unit 10 Ridgewood Industrial Park,

Uckfield, East Sussex,

TN22 5QE England

Tel: +44 (0) 1825 749494

www.naval-military-press.com

www.nmarchive.com

This diary has been reprinted in facsimile from the original. Any imperfections are inevitably reproduced and the quality may fall short of modern type and cartographic standards.

© **Crown Copyright**
Images reproduced by permission of The National Archives, London, England, 2015.

Contents

Document type	Place/Title	Date From	Date To
Heading	WO95/2942/2		
Heading	56th Division 512th Field Coy R.E. Feb 1916-Apr 1919		
Heading	56 2/1 London Fd Coy R.G. Vol II		
War Diary	Needham Market	04/02/1916	19/02/1916
War Diary	Southampton	21/02/1916	21/02/1916
War Diary	Havre	22/02/1916	23/02/1916
War Diary	Hocquincourt	24/02/1916	24/02/1916
War Diary	Berteaucourt	27/02/1916	11/03/1916
War Diary	Beauval	12/03/1916	12/03/1916
War Diary	Honval	14/03/1916	14/03/1916
War Diary	Duisans	27/03/1916	12/04/1916
War Diary	Honval	13/04/1916	23/04/1916
War Diary	Ivergny	26/04/1916	02/05/1916
War Diary	Souastre	03/05/1916	03/05/1916
War Diary	Sailly	04/05/1916	31/05/1916
Heading	Account at Digging Operations 19/5-28/5/1716		
Miscellaneous	Re Report Of Operations Of New Advanced Trench	28/05/1915	28/05/1916
Diagram etc	Diagram		
Miscellaneous	O.C. 8th Battn Middlesex Regt. Souastre.	28/05/1916	28/05/1916
Miscellaneous	Report Operation No.25	27/05/1916	27/05/1915
Miscellaneous	Report On New Front Line RE Operation	28/05/1916	28/05/1916
War Diary	Sailly	11/06/1916	22/07/1916
Heading	56th Divisional Engineers 2/1st London Field Company R.E August 1916		
War Diary	Sailly	15/08/1916	16/08/1916
War Diary	Doullens	19/08/1916	22/08/1916
War Diary	Heirment	23/08/1916	23/08/1916
War Diary	Neuf Moulins	23/08/1916	30/08/1916
Heading	56th Divisional Engineers 2/1st London Field Company R.E. September 1916		
War Diary	Neuf Moulin	02/09/1916	03/09/1916
War Diary	Vaux Sur Somme	04/09/1916	26/09/1916
Miscellaneous	Report On Work Done		
Miscellaneous	A Form Messages And Signals.		
War Diary	N Of Bronfay Farm	03/10/1916	08/10/1916
War Diary	E Of Trones Wood	09/10/1916	09/10/1916
War Diary	The Citadel	11/10/1916	12/10/1915
War Diary	Yzeux	12/10/1916	20/10/1916
War Diary	Erondelle	22/10/1916	23/10/1916
War Diary	Estaires	25/10/1916	28/10/1916
War Diary	Laventie	01/11/1916	01/03/1917
War Diary	Grand Pacquat	02/03/1917	02/03/1917
War Diary	Les Amusories	03/03/1917	03/03/1917
War Diary	Sains Lez Pernes	04/03/1917	04/03/1917
War Diary	Fresnoy	05/03/1917	05/03/1917
War Diary	Hauteville	06/03/1917	06/03/1917
War Diary	Boffles	06/03/1917	07/03/1917
War Diary	Ivergny	11/03/1917	22/03/1917
War Diary	Agny	23/03/1917	20/04/1917
War Diary	Coigneux	23/04/1917	24/04/1917

Type	Location	Start	End
War Diary	Guoyen Atois	26/04/1917	26/04/1917
War Diary	Simencourt	28/04/1917	28/04/1917
War Diary	Arras	29/04/1917	29/04/1917
Miscellaneous	56th Division		
War Diary	Arras	30/04/1917	21/05/1917
War Diary	Warlus	24/05/1917	28/05/1917
War Diary	Simencourt	01/06/1917	21/06/1917
War Diary	Achicourt	01/07/1917	03/07/1917
War Diary	Guoyen Artois	04/07/1917	04/07/1917
War Diary	Sombrin	05/07/1917	22/07/1917
War Diary	Houvigneul	23/07/1917	23/07/1917
War Diary	Serques	24/07/1917	27/07/1917
War Diary	Sombrin	29/07/1917	29/07/1917
War Diary	Serques	01/08/1917	05/08/1917
War Diary	Noordpeene	06/08/1917	06/08/1917
War Diary	Steenvoorde East	07/08/1917	12/08/1917
War Diary	New Dickebusch Camp	13/08/1917	15/08/1917
War Diary	Segard Chateau	16/08/1917	18/08/1917
War Diary	Ottawa Camp	18/08/1917	20/08/1917
War Diary	Busseboom	21/08/1917	25/08/1917
War Diary	Nordpeene	26/08/1917	26/08/1917
War Diary	Bleue Maison	26/08/1917	30/08/1917
War Diary	Beaulencourt	02/09/1917	04/09/1917
War Diary	Le Bucquiere	07/09/1917	22/11/1917
Diagram etc	Diagram		
War Diary		22/11/1917	30/11/1917
War Diary	Fremicourt	01/12/1917	02/12/1917
War Diary	Beaulencourt	03/12/1917	03/12/1917
War Diary	Simencourt	04/12/1917	05/12/1917
War Diary	Ecoivres	06/12/1917	07/12/1917
War Diary	Ecurie	08/12/1917	11/12/1917
Heading	2/1 London Fd Coy RE Vol III		
War Diary	Ecurie	10/12/1917	21/12/1917
War Diary	St Catherine	21/12/1917	08/01/1918
War Diary	Roberts Camp	13/01/1918	11/02/1918
War Diary	St Catherine	12/02/1918	21/02/1918
Heading	War Diary 512th (London) Field Company R.E March 1918		
War Diary	St Catherine	01/03/1918	31/03/1918
War Diary	56th Divisional Engineers 512th (London) Field Company R.E April 1918		
War Diary	Anzin	01/04/1918	05/04/1918
War Diary	Estree Couchie	06/04/1918	06/04/1918
War Diary	Agnez Les	07/04/1918	07/04/1918
War Diary	Duisans	07/04/1918	07/04/1918
War Diary	Berneville	07/04/1918	13/07/1918
War Diary	Habarcq	14/07/1918	14/07/1918
War Diary	Houvin H	15/07/1918	15/07/1918
War Diary	Beugin	16/07/1918	23/07/1918
War Diary	Batus	01/08/1918	01/08/1918
War Diary	Arras	05/08/1918	17/08/1918
War Diary	Ambrines	18/08/1918	18/08/1918
War Diary	Sars Les Bois	20/08/1918	20/08/1918
War Diary	Grand Rullecourt	21/08/1918	21/08/1918
War Diary	Gaudiempre	22/08/1918	22/08/1918
War Diary	Blaireville	23/08/1918	30/09/1918

War Diary	Marquion	05/10/1918	01/11/1918
War Diary	Noyelles	02/11/1918	02/11/1918
War Diary	Thiant	04/11/1918	04/11/1918
War Diary	Saultain	05/11/1918	05/11/1918
War Diary	Sebourquiaux	06/11/1918	08/11/1918
War Diary	Fme De Seigneur	09/11/1918	09/11/1918
War Diary	Ruinsette	10/11/1918	10/11/1918
War Diary	Lescommunes	12/11/1918	29/11/1918
War Diary	Villers Sire Nicole	03/12/1918	31/12/1918
War Diary	Villers Sire Nicole	04/01/1919	28/01/1919
War Diary	Villers Sire Nicole	01/02/1919	17/02/1919
War Diary	Cuesmes	18/02/1919	30/04/1919
Heading	2/1 London Fd Coy R.E 56 Feb Vol I		

WO 95/2942/2

56TH DIVISION

512TH FIELD COY R.E.

FEB 1916 – APR 1919.

56

2/1 London 3rd Coy
R.E.

Vol II

Army Form C. 2118.

WAR DIARY
or
INTELLIGENCE SUMMARY.
(Erase heading not required.)

2/1st London Field Coy RE (TF)

Instructions regarding War Diaries and Intelligence Summaries are contained in F.S. Regs., Part II. and the Staff Manual respectively. Title pages will be prepared in manuscript.

Place	Date	Hour	Summary of Events and Information	Remarks and references to Appendices
NEEDHAM MARKET	4/2/16	10 AM	Inspection by Brig Genl A.W.ROPER. C.B. R.E. (Inspector R.E.)	OMSJ
"	19/2/16	10 AM	Inspection by G.O.C. 58th London Division.	OMSJ
SOUTHAMPTON	22/2/16		Moved in two trains 2.50 A.M. & 4.50 A.M. & embarked in S.S. MAIDAN & S.S. CONNAUGHT Major O.R.D. JOHNSTONE, Capt R. ANNAN, Lieut E.L. MARTIN, J.T.F. HENDERSON, 2nd Lieuts D.E. CLERK & H.A. SCOTT. 223 Other Ranks, 79 horses + mules 19 vehicles + 33 bicycles.	OMSJ
HAVRE	22/2/16		French Interpreter, le Marquis d'ALBON reported for duty. Disembarked & marched to Docks Rest Camp.	OMSJ
HAVRE	23/2/16	2.20 PM	Entrained at Gare Maritime.	OMSJ
HOCQUINCOURT	24/2/16	6 A.M.	Arrived PONT REMY 6 A.M. Very frosty & slippery. Marched to billets HOCQUINCOURT.	OMSJ
BERTEAUCOURT	27/2/16	7 A.M.	Roads very greasy. Marched into billets BERTEAUCOURT & join 167th Brigade Group.	OMSJ

O.M.S.Munroe
Major R.E.(T.F)
O.C. 2/1st London Field Coy R.E.

Army Form C. 2118.

WAR DIARY
or
INTELLIGENCE SUMMARY. 2/1st London Field Coy RE (T.F.)
(Erase heading not required.)

Instructions regarding War Diaries and Intelligence Summaries are contained in F. S. Regs., Part II. and the Staff Manual respectively. Title pages will be prepared in manuscript.

Place	Date	Hour	Summary of Events and Information	Remarks and references to Appendices
BERTEAUCOURT	11/3/16		nil	Army
BEAUVAL	12/3/16		Moved by road into billets at BEAUVAL	Army
HONVAL	14/3/16		Moved by road into billets at HONVAL	Army
DULSANS	4/3/16		Two sections under Capt ANNAN, Lieut MARTIN and Lieut SCOTT to ARRAS (attached to 14th Divisional R.E.) Billets in ARRAS.	Army
			Remainder to DULSANS & report to O.C. VI Corps. Officers Major JOHNSTONE, Lieut HENDERSON + Lieut CLERK. Huts.	Army
	28/3/16		French Interpreter d'ALBON remains at HONVAL, attached 2/2nd London Fd Coy, of which two sections (Capt LAIRD) take over R.E. services for 167 & 169th Inf Bdes Works visited & repairs commenced on 1st line & 2nd position under C.E. VI Corps	Army

O M Johnstone
Maj RE (TF)
O.C. 2/1st London Field Coy RE (TF)

Army Form C. 2118.

WAR DIARY
or
INTELLIGENCE SUMMARY.
(Erase heading not required.)

2/1st London Field Coy RE (TF)

Instructions regarding War Diaries and Intelligence Summaries are contained in F. S. Regs., Part II. and the Staff Manual respectively. Title pages will be prepared in manuscript.

Place	Date	Hour	Summary of Events and Information	Remarks and references to Appendices
DUISANS	1/4/16		2 Sections on Fieldworks 2nd Position under C.E. VI Corps with working parties from 5th Division. Baths. 2 Sections attached 14th Divn working in front line ARRAS.	OMJ
"	12/4/16		Capt ANNAN Lieut MARTIN & 2nd Lieut SCOTT & Sections 1 & 2 proceed from ARRAS to SARS-LES-BOIS	OMJ
"	13/4/16		Lieut MARTIN & No 2 Section from SARS-LES-BOIS to LE CAUROY for work under C.R.E. H.Q. & Sections 3 & 4, relieved by 2/2nd London Field Coy at DUISANS, after handing over work etc.	
HONVAL			proceed to HONVAL, Major ORR JOHNSTONE Lieut HENDERSON & 2nd Lieut CLERK	OMJ
"	14/4/16		Searchlight apparatus & 5 attendants attached for work under C.E. VI Corps at AVESNES.	OMJ
"	22/4/16		Lieut H.M. HIGNETT 1/5th Cheshire Regt attached to visit & report for duty.	OMJ
"			Searchlight party (5 O.R.) & Apparatus rejoin from VI Corps.	OMJ
IVERGNY	26/4/16		H.Q. & Sections 3 & 4 move from HONVAL to billets in IVERGNY.	OMJ
"	27/4/16		2 Lieut H.A.SCOTT & No 1 Section from SARS-LES-BOIS rejoin unit at IVERGNY.	OMJ

G.W. Johnstone
Major RE (TF)
O.C. 2/1st London Field Coy RE (TF)

56

Army Form C. 2118.

WAR DIARY
or
INTELLIGENCE SUMMARY.
(Erase heading not required.)

2/1st London Field Coy RE (TF)

Instructions regarding War Diaries and Intelligence Summaries are contained in F.S. Regs, Part II. and the Staff Manual respectively. Title pages will be prepared in manuscript.

Army Form 4

Place	Date	Hour	Summary of Events and Information	Remarks and references to Appendices
IVERGNY	1/5/16		R.E. Work in hand for 169th Inf Bde Group handed over to 1st Edinburgh Field Coy R.E. at SARS-LES-BOIS	Only
"	2/5/16		Lieut H.M. HIGNETT 1/5th Durham Regt. leaves to rejoin his unit.	Only
SOUASTRE	3/5/16		Move to Huts in SOUASTRE. Lieut MARTIN + No 2 Section join unit from C.R.E. LECROROY	Only
SAILLY	4/5/16		Move to SAILLY. H.Q. + Sections 1 + 2, Major JOHNSTONE + Lieut MARTIN, to SAILLY	Only
			Sections 3 + 4, Capt ANNAN, Lieut HENDERSON + Lieut CLERK, to HEBUTERNE	Only
			Transport, 2/Lieut SCOTT, to BAYENCOURT	Only
"	19/5/16		No 1 Section, 2/Lieut SCOTT move to billets HEBUTERNE (with Nos 3 + 4 Sections)	Only
"	22/5/16		167th Inf Bde relieved by 169th Inf Bde in Front line.	Only
"	23/5/16		Night-Operations commenced. About 1600 yds front line advanced about 400 yds	Only
"	26/5/16	(4.30PM)	SAILLY shelled	} into wire in front also Support + Communication Trenches dug — see Reports attached hereto
"	27/5/16	(12.30PM)	SAILLY again shelled	Appendix 1
"	31/5/16		Night Operations completed.	Only
			Transport moves from BAYENCOURT to J.3.a.b. N of road COIGNEUX-SOUASTRE	

O.W. Johnstone
Maj R.E (TF)
O.C. 2/1st London Field Coy R.E (TF)

T2134. Wt. W708-776. 500000. 4/15. Sir J.C. & S.

Accounts
of Digging
Operation

19/5 – 28/5/1716

"C" Sector (1)

RE. REPORT OF OPERATIONS OF NEW ADVANCED TRENCH.

MAP REF 57D N.E. 3 & 4 (PARTS OF)
$\overline{10.000}$

At 9.30 P.M. on 19.6.16 I reconnoitred ground for new advanced trench on a front of 450 YDS. The left flank resting on GOMMECOURT ROAD & the right flank in the Valley to the South of No 1 SAP K10B25. I also got into communication with 1/7th Middx Reg on the left & 1/8th Middx Reg on the right.

The proposed line of trenches was sighted on the convex slope of the hill following the curve round & then running straight for South end of "Z" Hedge.

The new trench was kept slightly up the hill on the

ground lower appeared to be liable to be slightly water logged.

On the night of 25th – 26th the new front line was pegged & stringed on the line above sighted.

On the night of 26th – 27th the new front line was taped & ground was reconnoitered for Support line & Communication Trenches when it was found that old rifle pits could be converted into new communication trench. Ground was also reconnoitered for communication & fire trench from Sap No 2.

Communication trench was sighted from Sap No 2 to top of May Bush bank when fire trench was sighted behind hedge to give an enfilade fire to the north. This trench placed to be at about 2 ft from edge of

(3)

bank which is also connected to new front line by communication trench.

Takes out passage through wire in front of Tup N⁰ 2.

On the night of 27ᵗʰ–28ᵗʰ
Ht above Puppet line & communication trench was taped

A. D. Scott
2ⁿᵈ Lieut
4ᵗʰ Lovatts Scouts.

27.5.16.

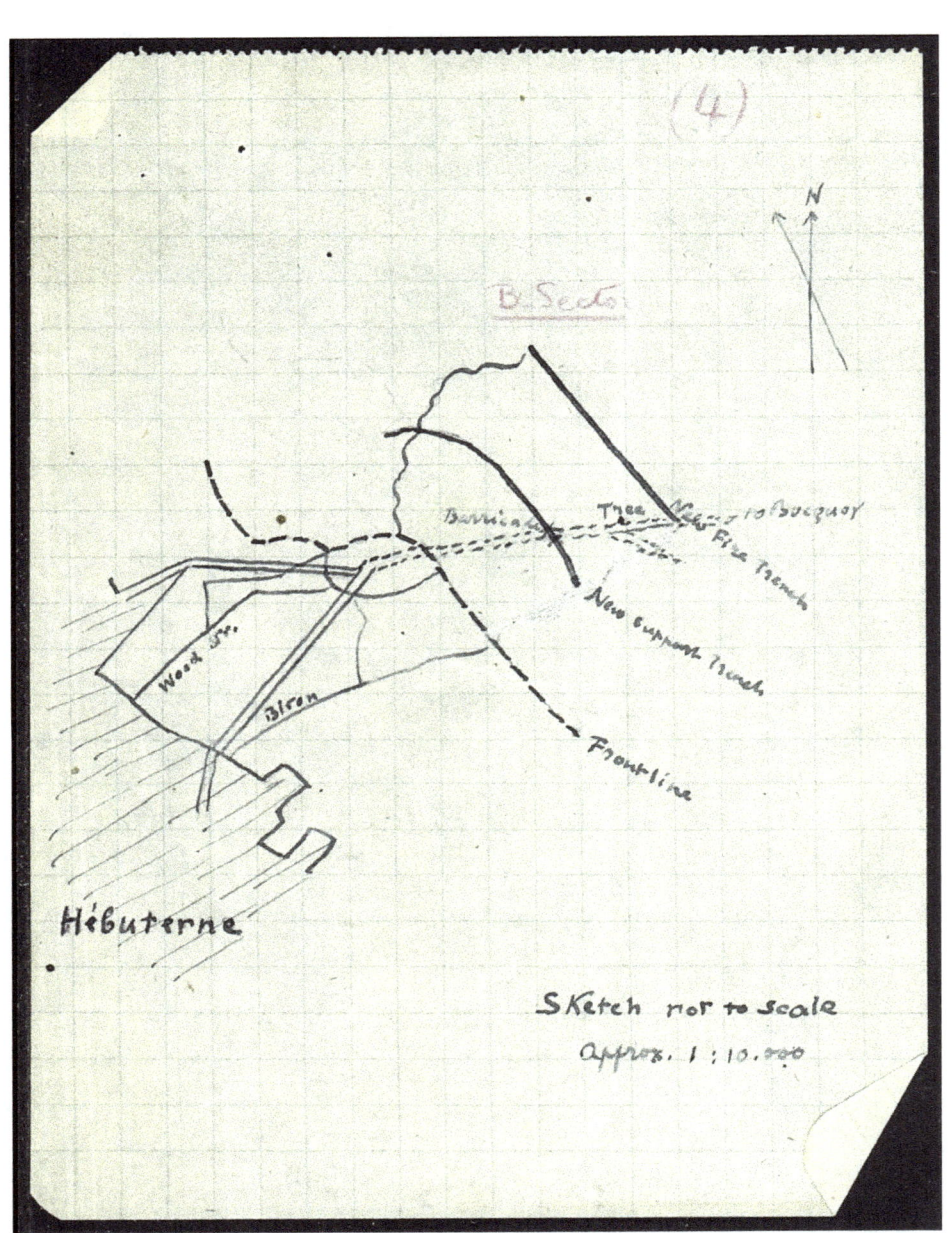

Copy "B" Sector (1)

O.C.
  8th Battn. Middlesex Regt
     SOUASTRE.   28/5/1916.

Sir,
    Map Ref 57D NE 3 & 4 (parts of)
$\frac{1}{100,000}$.

    Having been attached to your command for operations of the nights of 25/26th and 27th inst, I have the honour to report as follows:-
    On the night of the 25th inst I reported at your HQrs at HEBUTERNE to join taping party under Captain Peak, 8th Battn. Middlesex Regt. to set out proposed new trench from a point 100 yards EAST of line of fork on BUCQUOY ROAD to a point at K10b.46 at which point junction would be effected with 1/3 London Regt. and at starting point with 1/ London Regt.-

    We were unable to carry out the work for the following reasons:-
(1) The guide provided lost his way at the entrance to the trenches
(2) The trenches were blocked with working parties and as the 1/ London Regt. were using the same means of exit the party was about 110 strong near 3 hours were spent in reaching it. As the wire in front had not been cut the

head of the column was unable to advance owing to the presence of a hostile patrol which for this reason could not be dealt with.

(3) When another exit was reached the covering parties were returning and daylight prevented the work being carried out.

On the night of the 26th inst. we were at the point of exit at 9 p.m. prepared to leave but as the wire had to be cut our exit was delayed nearly 2 hours. I proceeded to at once set out and tape new fire trench and at 11.25 Capt Peake had the Battn. leading on to the work. When I had seen the Battn on the line I withdrew and acting under orders received from Brigade Major 167th Bde proceeded to reconnoitre the ground for proposed support trench to be dug on the night of the 27th. I reported to the Bde Major 167th Bde at 9 am 27th inst at HEBUTERNE and went with him to the front line to see the ground in daylight. I attended the conference at Bde HQrs at noon and received

(3)

instruction as to support trench.

At 9 p.m. with Capt. Peak I left the trench and proceeded to site and tape new support trench. The work was completed by 9.30. I remained on the BUCQUOY road with 4 sappers to supervise the construction of a barricade across the road. This was built to a height of 3'6" and a depth of two sandbags laid as headers. This work was seriously interfered with owing to machine guns and bursts of shell fire. At 1.30 a.m. under orders from Capt. Peak I started to lead the working parties in. During the operation the enemy opened machine gun and shell fire on our own and front line.

I attach sketch of operation not to scale.

I have the honour to be Sir
your obedient servant
(S) E. L. Hunter Lieut.
R.E.(T)
2/1st Fours Field Co. R.E.

"A" Sector (1)   7

Report on Operations 25-27/5/16.

MAP. REF.
　　　　SECRET 56/D/54 1/5000

Night of 25th - 26th
At 8.30 p.m. proceeded with covering party
of 1/1st London Rgt. up Strand St. C.T. We were
delayed in this trench by a working party.
On arriving at CROWS NEST we found
no wire had been cut. This work was
commenced at once. At 12 midnight a narrow
way was cut through wire. While the
covering party were moving out through
this opening a hostile patrol opened fire
which caused a little delay. After com-
municating with Major Glover 1/1st London
Rgt the covering party was moved down
the fire trench to Woman C.T. leading
to strong point. No opening in the wire
could be found. By this time it was
dawn and we returned to HEBUTERNE.

Night 26-27th
At 7.30 p.m. proceeded with covering party
of 1/1st London Rgt. up Woman St. C.T.
At 8-45 p.m. the covering party passed
out through wire at top of Woman St.

(2)

C.T. at LONE TREE we came on a hostile patrol but it was driven back. The taping of the new line was commenced. It was finished at 11.50 p.m, and the working parties afiled out immediately. At 12-45 A.M. I commenced to string line of New Support trench. This was finished at 1-45 A.M.

Night of 27-28.
I met covering party of 4th London Regt at top of Whitman St C.T. at 8.30 pm. Covering party moved out at 8-45 p.m. I commenced taping line of New C.T. immediately covering party had gone out. This taping was finished at 9.45 p.m. and working party was put to work at once. I proceeded afterwards to Northern C.T. leading to strong point where a party were employed making fire steps etc. This work was being carried out quite well. I returned to New C.T. and found everything there getting on favourably.

28/5/16.

Thos. G. Henderson
Lieut R.E.
2/1st London Field Coy R.E.

D Sector (?)

Report on New Front Line RE Operation

Map. Ref. 57^D NE 3 & 4 parts of 1/10000

On the night of 25th–26th inst I went out from N° 4 sap & reconnoitred ground for a new advanced trench.

The trenches were sited on a front of 690yds running from head of N° 4 sap round the slope of the hill to the N end of Z hedge & then following the Z hedge up to GOMMECOURT ROAD where I got in touch with the 3rd London Regt. The respective frontages were then pegged & stringed and are approx. 80 yds sap. 390 yds fire trench 40 yds communication trench 260 yds fire trench. Some wire was also cut outside N°4 sap. On the following night 26th–27th inst. the above frontage was taped & a new communication trench sited running from N° 3 sap to pt. K10a39 in Z hedge approx. 220 yds frontage.

On the night of 27th–28th inst the above mentioned communication trench was pegged & taped. A second communication & fire trench running from N° 2 sap to the May bush was also reconnoitred, pegged & taped. The approx frontages are 40 yds sap 160 yds communication trench 100 yds fire trench. Communication with the 3rd London Regt was established at the May bush. Some wire was cut and cleared at the head of No 2 sap & my work reported completed to the 7th Middlesex H.Q's at 11.5 p.m.

D E Clerk. 2/Lieut. RE.
2/1st London Field Co. RE.
28-5-16.

Army Form C. 2118.

WAR DIARY
or
INTELLIGENCE SUMMARY.
(Erase heading not required.)

2/1st London Field Coy R.E. (T.F.)

Vol 5

Instructions regarding War Diaries and Intelligence Summaries are contained in F.S. Regs., Part II. and the Staff Manual respectively. Title pages will be prepared in manuscript.

Place	Date	Hour	Summary of Events and Information	Remarks and references to Appendices
SAILLY	17/6/16		No 3 Section proceed to SAILLY & attached to 1/1st Edinburgh Field Coy	army
"	18/6/16		No 1 Section, 2nd Lieut HASCOTT, move from HEBUTERNE to billets GRENAS.	army
"	"		No 3 Section reporm unit & return to HEBUTERNE	army
"	19/6/16		No 2 Section Lieut E.L. MARTIN, move to ST AMAND. Billets.	army
"	21.6.16		Major O.R.B. JOHNSTONE leaves for England to Report to War Office	N.A.
"	"		Capt. R. ANNAN taken over command of the Company	T.A.
"	25.6.16		Coy HQ. Nos 3 & 4 Sections move to Billets in ST AMAND. Turning over work inhand to 1/1 Edinburgh Field Co	T.R.
"	27.6.16		No 1 Section Lieut H.A. SCOTT, rejoined Company from GRENAS	32 m
"	29.6.16		Capt R. ANNAN reveverts to Field Ambulance duty	
"	"		LIEVT. E.L. MARTIN took over command of the Company (pro tem)	4.2 m
"	30.6.16		No 1 Section Lieut H.A. SCOTT move from ST. AMAND to HEBUTERNE	4.2 m

E.L Martin
Lieut R.E.(T)
2/1 London Field Company.

WAR DIARY
INTELLIGENCE SUMMARY

(Erase heading not required.)

Army Form C. 2118.

2/1 London Field Co(R.E.)(T)

Place	Date	Hour	Summary of Events and Information	Remarks and references to Appendices
SAILLY	1/7/16		Coy HQ. No's 2, 3 & 4 Sections proceed to SAILLY	2 RW.
	2/7/16		2nd Lieut DE CLERK & No 2 Section proceed to HEBUTERNE to relieve 2nd Lieut H.A SCOTT No 1 Section	2 RW
			2nd Lieut H.A SCOTT & Yorks parts of No 1 Section upon road having had 2 casualties.	2 RW
			2nd Lieut SCOTT'S report attached.	2 RW
	3/7/16		2nd Lieut H.A SCOTT & No 1 Section proceed to HENU	2 RW
			Lieut J.T.F. HENDERSON to HEBUTERNE to relieve 2nd Lieut DE CLERK	2 RW
			2nd Lieut DE CLERK rejoined unit	2 RW
	5/7/16		No's 3 & 4 Sections proceed to HEBUTERNE. No 2 Section rejoind unit.	2 RW
	6/7/16		2nd Lieut DE CLERK proceed to HEBUTERNE. 2nd Lieut H.A SCOTT & No 1 Section rejoin unit.	2 RW
	7/7/16		Lieut E. L. MARTIN slightly wounded at duty.	2 RW
	10/7/16		Captain F. G. P. GEDGE & 2nd LIEUT J.A MERCER join for duty	2 RW
	15/7/16		Captain F.G.P.G.EDGE took over command of The Company.	J.M.
			2nd Lieut J.A MERCER proceeded to HEBUTERNE	J.M.
	17/7/16		Attached letter from GRE 38th Division conveying G.O.C's appreciation of good work done by Coy.	J.M.
	19/7/16		Draft of 50 men arrived from Base Havre	J.M.

J.M Mercey 2/ Lt 2/1 London Field Coy
OC 2/1 London Field Coy

Army Form C. 2118.

WAR DIARY
or
INTELLIGENCE SUMMARY.
(Erase heading not required.)

2/1 LONDON FIELD COMPANY

Place	Date	Hour	Summary of Events and Information	Remarks and references to Appendices
SAILLY	22.7.16		2ⁿᵈ Lieuts A.B. CHESTER & G. DYKE, J. ROBERTSON. D.S. COUSINS join for duty	July
			2ⁿᵈ Lieuts. G. DYKE, J. ROBERTSON. D.S. COUSINS proceeded to HEBUTERNE	July
			J. Nesly Capt RE b/.	
			re 2/1 London Field Company	

56th Divisional Engineers

2/1st LONDON FIELD COMPANY R. E.

AUGUST 1916

Army Form C. 2118.

INTELLIGENCE SUMMARY.
or
2/1 LONDON FIELD COMPANY
(Erase heading not required.)

Instructions regarding War Diaries and Intelligence Summaries are contained in F.S. Regs, Part II. and the Staff Manual respectively. Title pages will be prepared in manuscript.

Vol 1

Place	Date	Hour	Summary of Events and Information	Remarks and references to Appendices
SAILLY	15-8-16		2nd Lieut. CLERK and 16 men proceeded to LUCHEAUX on detachment	J. Ny.
	16-8-16		Le Marquis d'ALBON returned to French mission HENO for disposal.	J. Ny.
DOULLENS	19-8-16	8 AM	Company marched to DOULLENS arriving there 2.30.	J. Ny.
	22-8-16	8 AM	Company marched to HEIRMENT arriving there 12.30.	J. Ny.
HEIRMENT	23-8-16	7 AM	Company marched to NEUF MOULINS arriving 12.30 for special horsing	J. Ny.
NEUF MOULINS	23-8-16		Draft of five men arrived from 4th Base Depôt	J. Ny.
	29-8-16		2nd Lieut CLERK and 16 men returned	J. Ny.
	28-8-16		2 Officers, 24 other ranks attached from the following regiments for a trench pioneer course. 1/4 London, 1/12 London, 1/13 London, 1/14 London.	—
	30-8-16		Draft of three men arrived from 4th Base Depôt	J. Ny.

J. Nevedge
J. Nevedge
Capt. R.E.
O.C. 2/1 London Field Coy.

Signed to
CRE 1/9/16.
58 Divn.

56th Divisional Engineers

2/1st LONDON FIELD COMPANY R. E.

SEPTEMBER 1916.

WAR DIARY

INTELLIGENCE SUMMARY.
(Erase heading not required.)

Instructions regarding War Diaries and Intelligence Summaries are contained in F.S. Regs., Part II. and the Staff Manual respectively. Title pages will be prepared in manuscript.

2118.

2/9 Meaudon Field 10.9.12.16

Vol 3

Place	Date	Hour	Summary of Events and Information	Remarks and references to Appendices
	1916 September			
NEUF MOULIN	1		Lieut E.L.MARTIN, 2nd Lieut A.B.CHESTER took transport lines by road for VAUX SUR SOMME	John July
	2		Remainder of the Company lose by tram for VAUX SUR SOMME, detraining at CORBIE	July
	3		The Company marches by road to the Citadel (½ mile north of BRAY) into bivouacs	July
VAUX SUR SOMME	4			
	6		Capt F.G.P.GEDGE evacuated to Field Ambce, + Lieut E.L.MARTIN takes command	Run
			The Company moves into bivouacs north of BRONFAY FARM	Run
	10		2nd Lieut J.A.MERCER + W. H. Sexton attached to 167th Brigade for special operations	Run July
	11		Captain F.G.P.GEDGE returned to duty	July
	12		2nd Lieut J.A.MERCER returned to duty. A copy of his report is attached.	July
	14		The Company moves to S.W. of COMBLES for operations under 168th Brigade	
	2/		The Company withdrew from line to bivouacs north of BRONFAY FARM having been	
			continuously engaged in the operations from 14th. Having sustained	
			Casualties 2 killed, 19 wounded. See attached telegram from GOC General July	July
	13		Draft of 5 other ranks arrived from 48th Base Depot	July
	19		Draft of 5 other ranks arrived from 48th Base Depot	July
	26		Draft of 11 other ranks arrived from 48th Base Depot	July

Y.G. Murty
Colonel R.E.
O.C. 2/1 Lowestoft Coy

O.C. 2/1 London Fld. Co. R.E.

Report on Work done

At 4 p.m. I received orders from Brig. Gen. of 67 Brigade to wire the strong point at T.15.c.0.5. after it had been captured by 8th Mx. battalion.

I dumped pickets and barbed wire at the north corner of LEUZE WOOD and awaited the orders of the CO 8th Mx.

At 12 midnight the infantry commenced to bomb along the trench towards the strong point, but were held up just short of the road at T.15.c.0.5. Here they built a barricade, and a good deal of bombing took place. I went up to the barricade but it was impossible to go any further owing to bombing.

We made about 60 spheres of barbed wire & threw them over the barricade. We left at 5.30am & I reported to B.M. 67 Brigade.

12/9/16

118

"A" Form.   Army Form C. 2121
MESSAGES AND SIGNALS.   No. of Message _____

Prefix ___ Code ___ m.	Words	Charge	This message is on a/c of:	Recd. at ___ m.
Office of Origin and Service Instructions.	Sent			Date ___
	At ___ m.		___ Service.	From ___
	To ___			By ___
	By ___		(Signature of "Franking Officer.")	

TO { LXD6

| Sender's Number | Day of Month | In rep'y to Number | AAA |
| M.60. | 22nd | | |

Following is extract of wire from 14th Corps aaa Air photographs show that excellant work has been done by all Divisions in front line with a view to approaching nearer the enemy main positions and with this work the Corps Commander is much gratified aaa The new trench running from Middle Copse to T.15.d.11 will undoubtedly prove most useful as will also trench running from T.9.d.44 to T.15.b.52 aaa Extract ends aaa Divisional Commander is very pleased with work of last few nights planned and carried by Fatoh and executed by Labour and Lick.

From Longacre.
Place
Time
The above may be forwarded as now corrected.   (Z)
                                Censor.   Signature of Addressee or person authorised to telegraph in his name.
* This line should be erased if not required.

Army Form C. 2118.

WAR DIARY
INTELLIGENCE SUMMARY.
2/1st London Field Co. R.E. (2.5)
(Erase heading not required.)

Vol 9

Place	Date	Hour	Summary of Events and Information	Remarks and references to Appendices
N of BRONFAY FARM	3.10.16		The Company move by road to Trones Wood and on the evening 6 days both bad in the operations east of LESBOEUFS and sustained casualties, 3 men wounded	1/7/4 75/4
E of TRONES WOOD	9.10.16		The Company move to trones at THE CITADEL	75/4 75/4
THE CITADEL	11.10.16		Transport under Capt F.Q.P.GEDGE move to YZEUX via DAOURS by road	75/4
"	12.10.16		Remainder of Company under Lieut J.T.F.HENDERSON leave by motor bus for YZEUX	75/4
YZEUX	"		Draft of 5 other ranks arrived from 48th Base Depot	75/4
"	13.10.16		Captain F.Q.P.GEDGE to be MAJOR	75/4
"	"		Divisional Cards presented to 2399 Cpl MORRISON R, 2435 Cpl ROBERTS G.I and 2502 Cpl DALLINGER H by the C.R.E.	75/4
"	"		Draft of 13 other ranks awarded from 48th Base Depot	75/4
"	17.10.16		2399 Cpl MORRISON R. to awarded Military Medal for general good service during operations on the SOMME	75/4
"	"		Company move by road to ERONDELLE	5/4
"	20.10.16		2nd Lieut DE CLERK leaves for LAVENTIE to take over French tramways	75/4
ERONDELLE	22.10.16		2nd Lieut DE CLERK leaves for LAVENTIE to take over French tramways from 61st Field Co	75/4

over

WAR DIARY
or
INTELLIGENCE SUMMARY.
(Erase heading not required.)

Army Form C. 2118.

Place	Date	Hour	Summary of Events and Information	Remarks and references to Appendices
ERQUINGHEM	23.10.16		Company march to LONGPRÉ entraining there for ESTAIRES, arriving at 9.0 A.M. 24.10.16 & are in billets	4/hr.
ESTAIRES	25.10.16		Section Officers report to 1/3rd S.M. Field C.R.E. to take over work in hand.	4/hr.
"	28.10.16		Company move by road into billets at LAVENTIE & takes over work from 1/3rd S.M. Field C.R.E.	4/hr.

J. Mayr
MAJOR R.E. (T.F.)
O/C 2/1st LONDON FIELD COY R.E. (T.F.)

Army Form C. 2118.

WAR DIARY
or
INTELLIGENCE SUMMARY.
(Erase heading not required.)

2/1 London 1 Coy

Vol 10

Instructions regarding War Diaries and Intelligence Summaries are contained in F. S. Regs., Part II. and the Staff Manual respectively. Title pages will be prepared in manuscript.

Place	Date	Hour	Summary of Events and Information	Remarks and references to Appendices
LAVENTIE.	1-11-16		LIEUT. E. L. MARTIN. to be CAPTAIN dated 13-10-16	J.G.L.
"	3-11-16		Draft of 4 other ranks arrived from No 1. TERR. BASE DEPOT.	J.G.L.
	5-11-16		CAPTAIN E.L. MARTIN returned to Company from leave in ENGLAND.	J.G.L.
	11-11-16		2nd LIEUT. G. DYKE and No 3 SECTION proceed to Billets at NOUVEAU MONDE under orders of C.R.E.	J.G.L.
	12.11.16		MAJOR. F.P.G. GEDGE leaves for PARIS on special leave	J.G.L.
	13.11.16		CAPTAIN E.L. MARTIN takes over command of the Company	J.G.L.
	16.11.16		Draft of 3 other ranks arrived from No 1 TERR. BASE DEPOT.	J.G.L.
	16.11.16		2nd LIEUT. D.E. CLERK leaves for England on leave.	J.G.L.
	17.11.16		MAJOR F.P.G. GEDGE rejoins Company from Special leave in PARIS and resumes Command.	J.G.L.
	18.11.16		2nd LIEUT. G. DYKE and No 3. SECTION rejoin Company from NOUVEAU MONDE.	J.G.L.
	19.11.16		2nd LIEUT. J.A. MERCER and No 4 SECTION proceed to Billets at MERVILLE under orders of C.R.E.	J.G.L.
	23.11.16		Draft of 1 other rank arrived from No 1. TERR. BASE DEPOT.	J.G.L.
	23.11.16		2nd LIEUT. H.A. SCOTT leaves for England on leave.	J.G.L.
	26.11.16		2nd LIEUT. J.A. MERCER and No 4 SECTION rejoin Company from MERVILLE.	J.G.L.
	26.11.16		2nd LIEUT. D.E. CLERK returned to Company from leave in ENGLAND.	J.G.L.

F.G. Gedge.

2/1 London 20 C
Army Form C. 2118.
R.E.
Vol XI

WAR DIARY
or
INTELLIGENCE SUMMARY.
(Erase heading not required.)

Instructions regarding War Diaries and Intelligence Summaries are contained in F.S. Regs., Part II. and the Staff Manual respectively. Title pages will be prepared in manuscript.

Place	Date	Hour	Summary of Events and Information	Remarks and references to Appendices
LAVENTIE.	4/12/16		LIEUT J.T.F. HENDERSON leaves for England on leave	J.Gly
"	5/12/16		2/Lieut G. DYKE leaves for 1st ARMY SCHOOL.	J.Gly
"	7/12/16		Draft of 21 other ranks arrived from No 1. TERR. BASE DEPOT	J.Gly
"	10/12/16		MAJOR F.G.P. GEDGE leaves for England on leave	R.W.
"	"		CAPTAIN E.L. MARTIN takes over command of the Company	R.W.
"	"		2/LIEUT J. ROBERTSON and No 3 SECTION proceed to Billets at NOUVEAU MONDE under orders of C.R.E.	R.W.
"	15/12/16		LIEUT J.T.F. HENDERSON returned to Company from leave in England	R.W.
"	"		Draft of 2 other ranks arrived from No 1. TERR. BASE DEPOT	R.W.
"	21/12/16		2/LIEUT J. ROBERTSON and No 3 SECTION rejoin Company from NOUVEAU MONDE.	R.W.
"	"		2/LIEUT J. ROBERTSON and No 1. SECTION proceed to Billets at MERVILLE under orders of C.R.E.	R.W.
"	"		Draft of 6 other ranks arrive from No 1. TERR. BASE DEPOT.	R.W.
"	25/12/16		2/LIEUT J.A. MERCER leaves for England on leave	R.W.
"	"		MAJOR F.G.P. GEDGE returned from leave in England v resumed command of the Company	J.Gly
"	27/12/16		2/LIEUT A.B. CHESTER leaves for England on leave	J.Gly

J. Mudge Major
O.C. 2/1 London 2 Co

WAR DIARY
INTELLIGENCE SUMMARY

512
513 Fd Coy R.E.
London field C.E.
31 XI

Army Form C. 2118.

Place	Date	Hour	Summary of Events and Information	Remarks and references to Appendices
LAVENTIE	1/1/17		CAPTAIN E.L. MARTIN is awarded THE MILITARY CROSS for distinguished service in the field. London Gazette 1.1.1917.	July
"	1/1/17		2/LIEUT. J.A. MERCER returned to Company from leave in England.	July
"	2/1/17		2/LIEUT. H.A. SCOTT returned to Company from sick leave in England.	July
"	2/1/17		2/LIEUT. J. ROBERTSON and No 1 SECTION return Company from NERVIALE.	July
"	6/1/17		2/LIEUT. D.S. COUSINS leaves for England on leave.	July
"	7/1/17		2/LIEUT. A.B. CHESTER returned to Company from leave in England.	July
"	10/1/17		MAJOR F.G.P. GEDGE leaves for R.E. School of Instruction LE PARCQ.	July
"	11/1/17		CAPTAIN E.L. MARTIN. M.C. takes over command of the Company.	
"	14/1/17		2/LIEUT. G. DYKE rejoins Company from 1st ARMY SCHOOL	
"	14/1/17		2/LIEUT. G. DYKE and No 2 SECTION proceed to Billets at NOUVEAU MONDE under orders C.R.E.	
"	15/1/17		2/LIEUT. J. ROBERTSON transferred to Heavy Machine Corps and proceeds to BERMICOURT via St POL.	
"	16/1/17		2/LIEUT. G. DYKE leaves for England on leave.	You

J.H. Mudge

Army Form C. 2118.

WAR DIARY
or
INTELLIGENCE SUMMARY.
2/3 London Field C.R.E.
(Erase heading not required.)

Instructions regarding War Diaries and Intelligence Summaries are contained in F. S. Regs., Part II. and the Staff Manual respectively. Title pages will be prepared in manuscript.

Place	Date	Hour	Summary of Events and Information	Remarks and references to Appendices
LAVENTIE.	20.1.17		80 other ranks attached from the following regiments for a French Pioneer course. 1/4 London, 1/12 London, 1/13 London, 1/14 London.	2 Rwu
"	22.1.17		MAJOR F.G.P. GEDGE rejoins Company from R.E. School of Instruction LE PARCQ.	2 Rwu
"	22.1.17		2" LIEUT. H.C.G. PAICE 1/12 London Regiment attached to Unit reports for duty.	2 Rwu
"	22.1.17		LIEUT. J.T.F. HENDERSON reports to C.R.E. for duty as acting Adjutant.	2 Rwu
"	25.1.17		MAJOR F.G.P. GEDGE resumed command of the Company	J. Rly.
"	26.1.17		2" LIEUT H.C.G. PAICE & No 2 Section proceed to Billets at MERVILLE under orders of C.R.E.	J. Rly.
"	26.1.17		1. Officer attached from 1/12 London Regiment for a French Sewers course	J. Rly.
"	27.1.17		2" LIEUT. G. DYKE returned to Company from leave in England	J. Rly.
"	31.1.17		2" LIEUT. H.C.G. PAICE & No 2 Section rejoin Company from MERVILLE	J. Rly.

F.G.P. Gedge

T2134. Wt. W708—776. 500000. 4/15. Sir J.C.&S.

Army Form C. 2118.

WAR DIARY
of
INTELLIGENCE SUMMARY.
(Erase heading not required.)

Instructions regarding War Diaries and Intelligence Summaries are contained in F. S. Regs., Part II. and the Staff Manual respectively. Title pages will be prepared in manuscript.

572nd (London) Field Co. R.E.

Vol / 3

Place	Date	Hour	Summary of Events and Information	Remarks and references to Appendices
LAVENTIE	1/5/17		Under authority W.O. letter No. 9/Engineer/7611 (A.G.7) dated 8.1.17. title of Unit altered to 572nd (London) Field Co. R.E.	G.M.
"	2/5/17		MAJOR F.G.P. GEDGE reports to C.R.E. to take over duties of Actg. C.R.E.	9 Rum
"	3/5/17		CAPTAIN E.L. MARTIN. M.C. takes over Command of the Company	9 Rum
"	3/5/17		Company relieve the 416th (Edinburgh) Field Co. R.E. in the front line area between DRURY LANE and ERITH STREET, in the FAUQUISSART SECTION	9 Rum
"	3/5/17		2 Phases "B" other ranks attached from the following Regiments for "French Pioneer" Course. 12 (2nd) order, 15 (3rd) order, 14 (London) 116 (London)	9 Rum
"	5/5/17		Lieut E.G. COUSINS rejoined Company from sick leave in England	9 Rum
"	5/5/17		CAPTAIN E.L. MARTIN. M.C. leave for England on leave.	a Rum
"	5/5/17		LIEUT. J.A. MERCER takes over Command of the Company	fill
"	10/5/17		546403 SERGT. F. MORRISON awarded "CROIX DE GUERRE" for gallantry & devotion to duty in action	fill
"	13/5/17		2 LIEUT. J.A. MERCER to be 2nd Lieut. dated 13th October, 1916.	fill
"			Draft of 1 other rank arrived from R.E. Base Depot.	fill

J. Mercy

Army Form C. 2118.

WAR DIARY
or
INTELLIGENCE SUMMARY.
(Erase heading not required.)

Places	Date	Hour	Summary of Events and Information	Remarks and references to Appendices
LAVENTIE	24/5/17		MAJOR F G P GEDGE returned from C.R.E. and resumed command of the Company.	F.P.G.
"	25/5/17		CAPT. E L MARTIN M.C. returned to Company from leave in England.	F.P.G.
"	26/5/17		⅔ LIEUT. J. ROBERTSON rejoins Company from "D" Bat. Heavy Section. Machine Gun Corps.	F.P.G.
"	27/5/17		C.R.E. 49th Division inspects for taking over.	F.P.G.
"	28/5/17		MAJOR & CAPTAIN of 458th (N.R.) field C.R.E. report and take over R.E. work on hand.	F.P.G.

F.G.P. Gedge

Army Form C. 2118.

512 HP Co RE
Vol 14

WAR DIARY
or
INTELLIGENCE SUMMARY.
(Erase heading not required.)

Instructions regarding War Diaries and Intelligence Summaries are contained in F. S. Regs., Part II. and the Staff Manual respectively. Title pages will be prepared in manuscript.

Place	Date	Hour	Summary of Events and Information	Remarks and references to Appendices
LAVENTIE.	1/3/17		Company comes under orders of 169 Infantry Brigade for purposes of move.	yes
LAVENTIE.	1/3/17		Company move by road to GRAND PACQUAT into Billets arriving at 3.15 pm	yes
GRAND PACQUAT	2/3/17		Company move by road to LES AMUSOIRES into Billets arriving at Mid-day	yes
LES AMUSOIRES	3/3/17		Company move by road to SAINS LEZ PERNES into Billets arriving at 5.0 pm	yes
SAINS, LEZ PERNES	4/3/17		Company move by road to FRESNOY into Billets arriving at 11 o'clock	yes
FRESNOY.	5/3/17		Company move by road to HAUTEVILLE into Billets arriving at 1.30 pm	yes
HAUTEVILLE.	6/3/17		Company move by road to BOFFLES into Billets arriving at 1.0 pm	yes
BOFFLES.	6/3/17		Company transferred to 118th Railway Constructional Co. R.E. and proceeds	yes
"	6/3/17		2/Lieut. A.B. CHESTER. to ST. OMER.	yes
"			2/Lieut. D.F. CLERK. rejoins Company from LAVENTIE. having relieved from work as D.T.O.	yes
"	7/3/17		Company move by road to IVERGNY into Billets arriving at 3.0 pm.	yes
IVERGNY.	11/3/17		Company employed on improvements to area under orders C.E. VII CORPS.	yes
"	15/3/17		Lieut. G. DYKE + 40.4 SECTION proceed to Billets at COULLEMONT on detachment	yes
"	"		Lieut. J. ROBERTSON + 15 Sappers proceed to Billets at REBREUVIETTE on detachment	yes
"	15/3/17		Lieut. D.E. CLERK leaves to take over charge of C.R.E. Workshops at BAVINCOURT	yes

T2134. Wt. W708—776. 500000. 4/15. Sir J. C. & S.

WAR DIARY
of
INTELLIGENCE SUMMARY.
(Erase heading not required.)

Army Form C. 2118.

Place	Date	Hour	Summary of Events and Information	Remarks and references to Appendices
IVERGNY.	16/3/17		MAJOR. F.G.P. GEDGE evacuated to Field Ambulance. Captain E.L. MARTIN. M.C. takes command.	Q.2.W.
"	19/3/17		2nd LIEUT. G. DYKE & No.4 SECTION rejoin Company from COULLEMONT.	Q.2.W.
"	"		1st LIEUT. H.A. SCOTT + 6 men proceed to FREVENT in billets on detachment.	Q.2.W.
"	"		1st LIEUT. J. ROBERTSON + 15 men rejoin Company from REBREUVIETTE.	Q.2.W.
"	"		Company move by road to SIMENCOURT in billets arriving 6·0 pm.	Q.2.W.
"	2/3/17		1st LIEUT. G. DYKE & No.4 SECTION proceed to HUMBERCOURT in billets under orders of C.R.E.	Q.2.W.
"	22/3/17		Company move by road to AGNY in billets arriving 5·0 pm.	Q.2.W.
AGNY.	23/3/17		Company employed on road repairing under of C.R.E. 56 Division	Q.2.W.
"	"		Officers employed on reconnaissance of territory recently evacuated.	Q.2.W.
"	24/3/17		MAJOR. F.G.P. GEDGE rejoin Company from hospital.	Q.2.W.
"	"		1st LIEUT. G. DYKE & No.4 SECTION rejoin Company from HUMBERCOURT.	Q.2.W.
"	"		MAJOR. F.G.P. GEDGE resumed command of the Company.	H.M. / H.M.
"	7/3/17		1st LIEUT. H.A. SCOTT + 6 men rejoin Company from FREVENT.	H.M. / H.M.

Army-Form C. 2118.

WAR DIARY
~~INTELLIGENCE SUMMARY.~~
(Erase heading not required.)

Instructions regarding War Diaries and Intelligence Summaries are contained in F. S. Regs., Part II. and the Staff Manual respectively. Title pages will be prepared in manuscript.

Place	Date	Hour	Summary of Events and Information	Remarks and references to Appendices
AGNY.	30/3/17		Lieut. J.A. MERCER, ²/Lieut. G. DYKE, ²/Lieut D.S. COUSINS, ²/Lieut H.C.G. PAICE & Nos 1 & 4 Sections proceed to BEAURAINS.	24/4/17
				G. Mulye

Army Form C. 2118.

WAR DIARY
INTELLIGENCE SUMMARY
(Erase heading not required.)

5b 512 London Field Co. R.E.

Vol 15

Place	Date	Hour	Summary of Events and Information	Remarks and references to Appendices
AGNY	1/4/17		1 Officer + 81 other ranks attached from the following regiments for trench pioneer work - 4th London Regiment, 1/12 London Regiment, 1/13 London Regiment, 1/14 London Regiment	Jeln
"	4/4/17		2/Lieut. DE CLERK to be a/Lieut. dated 22.1.17	Jeln
"	4/4/17		2/Lieut. J. ROBERTSON levt. to D. Batt. M.G.C. Heavy branch as liaison officer between 56th D.N. Headquarters + tank Cos.	Jeln
"	8/4/17		Major F.G.P. GEDGE proceeds to BEAURAINS to take up battle position.	Jeln / Jeln
"	"		2/Lieut. H.A. SCOTT killed in action.	Jeln
"	"		2/Lieut. G. DYKE returns to Company from BEAURAINS + takes over temporary command of No 2 Section.	Jeln
"	9/4/17		2/Lieut. G. DYKE + Nos 2 + 3 Sections move into DIVISIONAL RESERVE in concentration area under C.R.E. MAP REF 51BS.N. Ed 4A 20.000 M.3 a H.5.	Jeln
"	"		Lieut DE CLERK rejoins Unit from BAVINCOURT + proceeds to concentration area + resumes command of No 3 Section	Jeln
"	"		"C" Company 1/5 CHESHIRE PIONEER BATT. come under orders of O.C. 512th R.E.	Jeln
"	"		LIEUT. J.A. MERCER, ¾LIEUT. D.S. COUSINS + 2/LIEUT H.C.G. PAICE, conducted strong points east of NEUVILLE VITASSE with mixed bodies of sappers, Cheshire pioneers +	Jeln

J.C. Murphy

Army Form C. 2118.

WAR DIARY
INTELLIGENCE SUMMARY.
(Erase heading not required.)

512 London Field C.o.E.

Place	Date	Hour	Summary of Events and Information	Remarks and references to Appendices
			Infantry Pioneer, see attached reports.	
	9.4.17		LIEUT JOLIFFE 115TH CHESHIRE PIONEERS arrived in NEUVRANG & consolidating	1/2 l/n
	10.4.17		TELEGRAPH TRENCH captured east of NEUVILLE VITASSE and attacked again. Sections employed in clearing roads on eastern side of captured terrain, at midnight the O.C. 2 Sections again came under command of C.R.E. "C" Company 15th Cheshire Pioneers left & Infantry Church Pioneers return to Brigade.	4/1/n
	11.4.17		Sections employed in opening up roads & dugouts in the HINDENBURG LINE.	2/2 l/n
	12.4.17		LIEUT. T.A. MERCER 2/LIEUT. D.S. COUSINS 2/LIEUT. H.C.G. PAICE + Nos 1 + 4 SECTIONS move forward to billets in NEUVILLE VITASSE. Sections employed opening up roads & dugouts in HINDENBURG LINE.	4/2 l/n
	13.4.17		MAJOR. F.G.P. GEDGE returned to Billet in AGNY	4/2 l/n
	15.4.17		2/LIEUT Q. DYKE + No 2 SECTION proceed to billets in NEUVILLE VITASSE	4/2 l/n
	17.4.17		LIEUT DE CLERK + No 3 SECTION proceed to billets in NEUVILLE VITASSE.	4/2 l/n
	19.4.17		LIEUTS J.A. MERCER + DECLERK 2/LIEUTS G. DYKE D.S. COUSINS + H.C.G. PAICE + Nos 1, 2, 3, 4 SECTIONS Return to billets at AGNY.	4/2 l/n

Army Form C. 2118.

WAR DIARY
or
INTELLIGENCE SUMMARY.
(Erase heading not required.)

Instructions regarding War Diaries and Intelligence Summaries are contained in F. S. Regs., Part II. and the Staff Manual respectively. Title pages will be prepared in manuscript.

512th (London) Field Coy. R.E.

Place	Date	Hour	Summary of Events and Information	Remarks and references to Appendices
AGNY	20.4.17		"C" in charge under Capt. E.L. MARTIN M.C. move to COIGNEUX by road via DAINVILLE	July
			HUMBERCAMPS & SOUASTRE	
			Remainder of Company under Major F.G.P. GEDGE leave by motor bus for COIGNEUX arriving 6 o'clock in into huts	July
COIGNEUX	23.4.17		Major F.G.P. GEDGE leaves for England on special leave.	9am
"	23.4.17		Captain E.L. MARTIN M.C. takes over command of the Company	9am
"	24.4.17		Company move by road to GUOY EN ATOIS into huts arriving 6 o'clock am	10am
GUOY EN ATOIS	26.4.17		Company move by road to SMIENCOURT into billets arriving 2.15 pm	4pm
SMIENCOURT	28.4.17		Lieut T.A. MERCER + DE.CLERK + ²Lieut H.C.G. PAICE report to 74 Field C.R.E. & take over billets no work as handed over.	30am
"	28.4.17		Company move by road to ARRAS into Billets arriving midday.	30am
ARRAS.	29.4.17		Billets slightly shelled, the Company had 2 casualties & chairs as result	30am

E. Martin

CAPTAIN R.E.
O.C. 512th (LONDON) FIELD COY. R.E.

C.R.E.
56th Division.

I have the honour to submit the following report on the work carried out by the Company during the last fortnight. During the week ending April 7th all the Sappers were engaged on clearing the roads through BEAURAINS, one party (No 4 SECT) under 2/LIEUT. G DYKE working for 7 consecutive nights were employed on clearing forward tracks & roads through MERCATEL & up to our front line. A party of No 1 SECTION under Lieuts MERCER & COUSINS cleared entrances to German dugouts in BEAURAINS. A further party of both sections opened up Wells under 2/LIEUT. PAICE. My transport established a battle dump in BEAURAINS. I established myself in BEAURAINS midday on the 8th instant.

At midnight the G.O.C

165th Brigade. placed 'C' Company 1/5TH CHESHIRES PIONEER BATT. commanded by LIEUT. JOLIFFE, and 20 other ranks Trench Pioneers from each of the Brigades Infantry Battalions, under the command of 2/LIEUT. BROCKHURST, under my command for the ensuing operations. At midday on the 9' instant I sent forward 2/LIEUT COUSINS with a mixed body of Sappers, Cheshires, & Pioneers, to dig & wire two strongpoints on the left flank of the RANGERS, who had by then carried the BLUE LINE. This work was completed by 6 pm. I also sent forward at midday LIEUT MERCER, 2/LIEUT PAICE & two Cheshire Subalterns with a larger body of men of a similar composition to establish 3 strongpoints on the Eastern side of NEUVILLE VITASSE, this work was satisfactorily completed by 10 pm. at 4 pm LIEUT. JOLIFFE went forward with a mixed body including Sappers to assist the LONDON SCOTTISH &

2.

of KENSINGTONS in reference to consolidating trenches in the HINDENBURG LINE east by north of NEUVILLE VITASSE. The whole of these strong points then forming a defensive flank for the left flank of the 56th DIVISION. This work was completed at 3.0 am on the 10th instant

At 11 o'clock am on the 10th instant I sent 2/LIEUT. COUSINS forward to clear a track for guns (18 pdrs) up to & through NEUVILLE VITASSE. This road was opened to transport at 6 pm to the eastern side of village.

LIEUT. MERCER & 2/LIEUT. PAICE opened up dugouts & wells in the village.

I established a forward dump in NEUVILLE VITASSE the same evening.

At midnight the composite body of troops was broken up & all bodies returned to their units.

I attach a report by CAPT MARTIN M.C. covering the work done during this period by Sections 2 & 3, under LIEUT. CLERK & 2/LIEUTS SCOTT & DYKE.

[margin note:] No report is sent in stated as finishing done by these sections in ?C.P.G.

4

I have to bring to your notice the names of the following Officers who have given me the most valuable assistance & who have carried out all the work entrusted to them.

  LIEUT. MERCER
  2/LIEUT. COUSINS.

both shewed great resource in siting the before mentioned strongpoints & made use of much enemy material. By so siting their points they were protected by enemy view.

  Both. LIEUT. JOLIFFE & 2/LIEUT. BROCKHURST gave me most loyal assistance.

  The following N.C.O's were indefatigable in pushing forward stores.

  54615?. C.S.M. GRANT.
  546040. /Cpl. GABBEDEY.

the former going forward at an early hour on Z day with SAPPER ABEL to reconnoitre for positions for forward dump. the latter /Cpl GABBEDEY loading &

5

taking forward 10 wagon loads of R.E. Material. The whole of this work being done under intermittent shell fire on the road.

It gives me the greatest pleasure in being able to report that without exception, all ranks under my command rose to the occasion. tired & wet they might have been, & where all worked so well, it is most difficult to select any special names for mention.

(Signed) J. G. Gedge

MAJOR R. E.
O/C 512th (LONDON) FIELD COY. R.E.

13/4/17.

Army Form C. 2118.

Vol 16

512th (London) Field Co. R.E.

WAR DIARY

of

INTELLIGENCE SUMMARY.

(Erase heading not required.)

Instructions regarding War Diaries and Intelligence Summaries are contained in F.S. Regs., Part II. and the Staff Manual respectively. Title pages will be prepared in manuscript.

Place	Date	Hour	Summary of Events and Information	Remarks and references to Appendices
ARRAS.	30/4/17		2/Lieuts G. DYKE & D.E. COUSINS & Nos 2+4 SECTIONS proceed to MAP REF 51B.S.N.3. Ld H^a O. 13 b 2.5 to be attached to 169th Infantry Brigade for work on advanced Battalion H.Q. and Aid Post.	
"	30/4/17		1 Corporal & 12 other ranks placed at disposal of Divisional Observation Officer for purpose of constructing Divisional Observer Dugout.	Q.R.W.
"	1/5/17		LIEUT D.E. CLERK & Nos 1 & 3 SECTIONS proceed to MAP REF 51B.S.N.2 Ld H^a N.11.a.7.7. for purpose of constructing advanced Bearer Post.	Q.R.W.
"	2/5/17		Horse standings moved to a point south of NEUVILLE VITASSE R^d between MAP REF 51B. N.N.3. E^d T^a. G.35.a.2.6. & G.35.a.5.1. by order of C.R.E. 56 DIV.	Q.R.W.
"	2/5/17		LIEUT D.E. CLERK & Nos 1 & 3 SECTIONS return to Billets at ARRAS.	Q.R.W.
"	2/5/17		LIEUT D.E. CLERK joins Nos 2 & 4 SECTIONS for operations.	Q.R.W.
"	2/5/17		LIEUT D.E. CLERK & 2/LIEUT G. DYKE & 2 & 4 SECTIONS come under orders of 169th Infantry Brigade for operations & are accommodated in trench at MAP REF. 51BS.N.2 E^d H^a N.17.d.7.7.	Q.R.W.
"	3/5/17		2/LIEUT G. DYKE wounded in action	Q.R.W.
"	3/5/17		2/LIEUT J. ROBERTSON proceeds to N.17.d.7.7. in place of 2/LIEUT G. DYKE wounded	Q.R.W.

T2134. Wt. W708—776. 500000. 4/15. Sir J. C. & S.

Army-Form C. 2118.

WAR DIARY
or
INTELLIGENCE SUMMARY.
(Erase heading not required.)

5/1st London Field C.R.E.

Instructions regarding War Diaries and Intelligence Summaries are contained in F.S. Regs., Part II. and the Staff Manual respectively. Title pages will be prepared in manuscript.

Place	Date	Hour	Summary of Events and Information	Remarks and references to Appendices
ARRAS	4/5/17		LIEUT. D.E. CLERK, 2/LIEUT. J. ROBERTSON + 2 Sections constructed rumoured strongpoint at MAP REF. 51B.S.W.2. 2ºH.A. O.13.d.x.9. Nº 546401 A/Sergt. W.T. NISBET + Nº 546026 CORPL. F.N. CORNWELL brought to notice of CR.E. 56th Dn for very fine work done during these operations.	R.L.W.
"	5/5/17		LIEUT. D.E. CLERK, 2/LIEUT J. ROBERTSON + Nºs 2 & 4 Sections return to Billets at ARRAS.	R.L.W.
"	11/5/17		2/LIEUT. D.S. COUSINS + Nºs. 2 + 4 Sections on night of 6/7/8/17 engaged in wiring the captured GERMAN WANCOURT LINE.	2 Runr
"	8/5/17		Draft of 5 other ranks arrived from R.E. Base Depot.	2 Rn
"	10/5/17		LIEUT. J.A. MERCER, 2/LIEUTS. D.E. COUSINS + J. ROBERTSON + Nºs 1, 2 & +4 SECTIONS move to MAP REF. SHEET 51B.S.W. N.9.c.3.5. & come under orders of G.O.C. 168th Infantry Brigade.	2 Runr
"	11/5/17		MAJOR F.G.P. GEDGE returned from leave in England & resumed command of the Company.	G.H.
"	11/5/17		LIEUT. D.E. CLERK + Nº 3 SECTION move to MAPREF. Sheet 51st S.W. N.9.c.3.5 & come under orders of G.O.C. 168th Infantry Brigade.	G.H.
"	12/5/17		MAJOR F.G.P. GEDGE and advanced H.Q. move to MAP REF. 51B S.W. N.9.c.3.5	G.H.

WAR DIARY
or
INTELLIGENCE SUMMARY.
(Erase heading not required.)

Army Form C. 2118.

512th (London) Field C.R.E.

Place	Date	Hour	Summary of Events and Information	Remarks and references to Appendices
ARRAS	night 12/13 5/17		LIEUT. J.A. MERCER & No 1 SECTION wired in front of trench from MAP. REF. 51B.S.W. O.8.a.2.8 to O.8.a.4.8	5/5/17
"	"		LIEUT. D.S. COUSINS & No 4 SECTION completed strong point at MAP. REF. 51B.S.W. O.8.a.3.7	5/5/17
"	"		2/LIEUT. J. ROBERTSON & No 2 SECTION reported to LOSR to form block at MAP REF. 51B.S.W. O.8.d. 10.05 but tactical situation did not permit work being done, and LIEUT. DE CLERK and No 3 SECTION reported to move it.	5/5/17
"	13/14		2/LIEUT. J. ROBERTSON & No 2 SECTION establish wire block across sunken road at MAP. REF. 51B.S.W. O.8.c.9.3	5/5/17
"	"		LIEUT. DE CLERK & No 3 SECTION carried material up to block ARRAS. CAMBRAI. ROAD in front of CAVALRY FARM about MAP REF. 51B.S.W. O.14.b.1.3. owing to light barrage of party becoming casualties no work was done, material being dumped at site of work. A large enemy party was observed moving forwards over foot.	5/5/17
"	14/15		Forward dump established at MAP. REF. 51B.S.W. O.8.a.2.4 & O.8.a.8.1.	5/5/17
"	15.5.17		Company came under orders of 167th Infantry Brigade	5/5/17

Army Form C. 2118.

WAR DIARY
or
INTELLIGENCE SUMMARY.
(Erase heading not required.)

512 Londonfield C.R.E.

Instructions regarding War Diaries and Intelligence Summaries are contained in F.S. Regs., Part II. and the Staff Manual respectively. Title pages will be prepared in manuscript.

Place	Date	Hour	Summary of Events and Information	Remarks and references to Appendices
ARRAS	August 15/8/16		2/Lieut D.S. COUSINS & No 4 SECTION erected 100 yards entanglement in front of SHRAPNEL TRENCH from MAP. REF. 51B.S.N. O.8.a.33. towards O.8.a.8.2. LIEUT J.A. MERCER & No 1 SECTION put in pickets along C.o.1. south of copse at MAP. REF. 51B.S.N. O.8. Central. Enemy activity prevented erection of wire & carrying task completed by Infantry failed to deliver material.	7/R.n
"	15/8/16		2/Lieut D.S. COUSINS returned to Billets at ARRAS & 2/LIEUT H.C.G. PAICE proceeded to MAP. REF. 51B.S.N. N.9.c.3.5.	7/R.n
"	August 17/8/16		Draft of 6 other ranks arrived from No 5 Reinforcement C.R.E.	7/R.n
"	"		Reconnaissance made by LIEUT J.A. MERCER DECLERK & 2/LIEUT J. ROBERTSON for Infantry Company H.Q.	7/R.n
"	18.8.17		No 54604 H.O. L/Corporal Gabtech.C. is awarded "Military Medal" for gallantry in the field	7/R.n
"	18.8.17		Lieut. H.C.G. PAICE evacuated to Field Ambulance sick	7/R.n
"	August 18/19		Advanced Infantry Company H.Q. constructed at MAP REF. 51B.S.N. O.14.a.10.35. & C.T. dug thereform to CAVALRY TRENCH under No 54643 Corp Reid. A.R.	7/R.n
"	18/19		2/LIEUT J. ROBERTSON & 16 SAPPERS stood by in 70CL TRENCH to put block in	7/R.n

Army Form C. 2118.

WAR DIARY
or
INTELLIGENCE SUMMARY.
(Erase heading not required.)

512th (London) Field C.R.E.

Instructions regarding War Diaries and Intelligence Summaries are contained in F.S. Regs., Part II. and the Staff Manual respectively. Title pages will be prepared in manuscript.

Place	Date	Hour	Summary of Events and Information	Remarks and references to Appendices
ARRAS.	18/4/17		captured portion of TOOL TRENCH, but did not work, as attack failed	J.M.
	19.5.17	night 10.P.M.	2/LIEUT. J ROBERTSON + No 2 + 4 SECTIONS return to Billets in ARRAS	J.M.
"			LIEUT. DE CLERK completed excavation for Coy. H.Q. at MAR REF 51B.S.W.O.7 & 8.2 & stood by to assist in consolidation of captured portion of HOOK TRENCH but was not required as attack failed.	J.M.
"			The Company sustained total casualties 1Officer Wounded 5 or Killed 11 or Wounded during these operations	J.M.
"	20.5.17		MAJOR. P.G.P.GEDGE. LIEUT. T.A. MERCER + DE CLERK + Nos 1 + 3 SECTIONS return to Billets in ARRAS	J.M.
"	21.5.17		Company move by road to NARLOS and HUTS + TENTS arriving 11oclock A.M.	J.M.
NARLUS.	24.5.17		Company move by road to SIMENCOURT into Billets arriving midday	J.M.
"	26.5.17		LIEUT. DE CLERK + 2/LIEUT. J. ROBERTSON proceed to England on leave.	J.M.
"	28.5.17		Draft of 10 other ranks arrived from No 2 Reinforcement C.R.E.	J.M.
			Major. P.G.P.Gedge mentioned in despatches (London Gazette April 5th 1917	J.M.

J.M. Murtey
Major V. Major R.E.Co.

T2134. Wt. W708—776. 500000. 4/15. Sir J. C. & S.

Army Form C. 2118.

WAR DIARY
INTELLIGENCE SUMMARY
(Erase heading not required.)

512th London Field C.R.E.

Place	Date	Hour	Summary of Events and Information	Remarks and references to Appendices
SIMENCOURT	1.6.17		2/LIEUT. E.L. MARTIN M.C. (Hon'y Captain) to be Acting Captain dated 26 August 1916.	J.E.W.
"	1.6.17		2/LIEUT V.L. FARFAN joins for duty	J.E.W.
"	2.6.17		Draft 3 other ranks arrived from No.3 Reinforcement C.R.E.	J.E.W.
"	2.6.17		Commission undertaken by C.R.E. + Divisional cards presented to No. 546041 a/Serg. N.T. NISBET + No. 546040 a/Serg. E. GABBEDY	J.E.W.
"	3.6.17		Draft 30 other ranks arrived from No.6 Reinforcement C.R.E.	J.E.W.
"	4.6.17		Company inspected by G.O.C. 56th Division + No. 546040 a/Serg. E. GABBEDY decorated with "Military Medal" Ribbon by G.O.C. 56 Division. see attached remarks by G.O.C.	J.E.W.
"	4.6.17		Draft 8 other ranks arrived from No.2 Reinforcement C.R.E.	J.E.W.
"	7.6.17		Draft 2 other ranks arrived from No.5 Reinforcement C.R.E	J.E.W.
"	7.6.17		No. 546006 Sergt T.W. HAYDAY awarded "Meritorious Service Medal"	J.E.W.
"	7.6.17		CAPTAIN J.T.F. HENDERSON is awarded THE MILITARY CROSS for distinguished service in the field order Gazette 4.6.1917	J.E.W.
"	10.6.17		2/LIEUT R.W. JAMES 1/12 LONDON REGT. attached to Unit reports for duty.	J.E.W.
"	10.6.17		2/LIEUT D.S. COUSINS reports to 478th FIELD C.R.E. to take over work in hand.	J.E.W.

Army Form C. 2118.

WAR DIARY
or
INTELLIGENCE SUMMARY.
(Erase heading not required.)

512th London Field Coy. R.E.

Instructions regarding War Diaries and Intelligence Summaries are contained in F. S. Regs., Part II. and the Staff Manual respectively. Title pages will be prepared in manuscript.

Place	Date	Hour	Summary of Events and Information	Remarks and references to Appendices
	10.6.17		MAJOR F.G.P. GEDGE, Headquarters + transport move to MAP REF. 1/40.000 SHEET 51B G.32.f.3.2. and 6 Bivouac + remainder of Company under CAPTAIN E.L. MARTIN M.C. move to MAP REF. 1/40.000 SHEET 51B N.8.d.S.S. and Bivouac.	Ap.1
	11.6.17		Draft 22 other ranks arrived from No. 5 Reinforcement 6.26	Ap.3
	11.6.17		LIEUT. DE CLERK + 2/LIEUT. J. ROBERTSON rejoin from leave in England	Ap.1.A
	11.6.17		Draft 6 other ranks arrived from No. 2 Reinforcement 6.26	Ap.1.A
	15.6.17		Draft 1 other rank arrived from No. 2 Reinforcement 6.26	Ap.1.A
	19.6.17		Draft 2 other ranks arrived from No. 2 Reinforcement 6.26	Ap.1.A
	21.6.17		Draft 2 other ranks arrived from R.E. Base Depot, ROUEN.	Ap.1.A
	21.6.17		MAJOR F.G.P. GEDGE + Headquarters move to MAP REF. 1/40.000 SHEET 51B N.8.d.S.S. and Bivouac + CAPTAIN. E.L. MARTIN M.C. proceeds to Obandons lines. During period in the line the Company were engaged round the clock on mined cured DUGOUTS at MAP REF. 1/40.000 SHEET 5.P.5.N. O.13.K. O.C. SADDLE TRENCH O.13.b.35. "S" GORDON CRATER C.T. + O.13.d.6.3. LOCK TRENCH	Ap.1

F.G. Gedge MAJOR R. E.
O/C 512th (LONDON) FIELD COY. R.E.

Army Form C. 2118.

512 (London) Field Co RE

WAR DIARY
~~INTELLIGENCE~~ SUMMARY.
(Erase heading not required.)

Instructions regarding War Diaries and Intelligence Summaries are contained in F. S. Regs., Part II. and the Staff Manual respectively. Title pages will be prepared in manuscript.

Place	Date	Hour	Summary of Events and Information	Remarks and references to Appendices
CHOCQUES	1/7/15		MAJOR F.O.P. GEDGE, Headquarters & No 4 SECTION move to Morve/wes at MAP REF. SHEET. 51.C. G.30 + 3.2.	/5/15
"	3/7/15		Lieuts J.A. MERCER, DE CLERK & Lieuts D.S. COUSINS, J. ROBERTSON, V.L. FARFAN & P.L. JAMES & Nos 1, 2 & 3 SECTIONS rejoin the Company at Morve/wes & Company move by road to GUOY EN ARTOIS arriving 6 o'clock pm into billets.	3/5/15
GUOY EN ARTOIS	4/7/15		Company move by road to SOMBRIN arriving 11 o'clock am into billets.	4/5/15
SOMBRIN	5/7/15		²/Lieut. D.S. COUSINS & S.O.R proceed to REST CAMP at SAINT VALERY SUR SOMME.	5/5/15
"	15/7/15		Lieut. J.A. MERCER proceeds on leave to ENGLAND.	15/7/15
"	20/7/15		²/Lieut. P.L. JAMES proceeds on leave to ENGLAND.	20/7/15
"	21/7/15		Lieut. DE CLERK proceeds to EPERLECQUES with advance billeting parts for DIV. HQ.	21/7/15
"	22/7/15		Company move by road to HOUVIGNEUL arriving midday into billets.	22/7/15
HOUVIGNEUL	23/7/15		Company march to PETIT HOUVIN entraining there for SERQUES detraining at SAINT OMER & move to SERQUES arriving 2.30am 24/7/15 into billets.	24/7/15
SERQUES	24/7/15		Lieut. DE CLERK rejoins the Company.	24/7/15
"	25/7/15		²/Lieut. D.S. COUSINS & S.O.R rejoins Company from REST CAMP.	25/7/15
"	27/7/15		Lieut. J.A. MERCER rejoins Company from leave in ENGLAND.	27/7/15

J.A. Mercer

Army Form C. 2118.

WAR DIARY
INTELLIGENCE SUMMARY
(Erase heading not required.)

512th London Field C.R.E.

Instructions regarding War Diaries and Intelligence Summaries are contained in F.S. Regs., Part II. and the Staff Manual respectively. Title pages will be prepared in manuscript.

Place	Date	Hour	Summary of Events and Information	Remarks and references to Appendices
SOMBRIN	29/7/15		Company employed in Training. Draft 1 other rank arrived from R.E. Base Depot.	H.M.

J. Meely
MAJOR R.E.
O/C 512th (LONDON) FIELD COY. R.E.

Army Form C. 2118.

WAR DIARY
INTELLIGENCE SUMMARY.
(Erase heading not required.)

Instructions regarding War Diaries and Intelligence Summaries are contained in F. S. Regs., Part II. and the Staff Manual respectively. Title pages will be prepared in manuscript.

512th (London) Field Coy.

J.M./19

Place	Date	Hour	Summary of Events and Information	Remarks and references to Appendices
SERQUES.	1.8.17		MAJOR F.G.P. GEDGE leaves for PARIS on leave & CAPT. E.L. MARTIN. M.C. takes over command of the Company.	9 R.M.
"	1.8.17		2nd LIEUT. P.L. JAMES rejoins Company from leave in England.	9 R.M.
"	3.8.17		2nd LIEUT. D.S. COUSINS & No.4 SECTION proceed to V Army Musketry Camp NORTBECOURT. under orders of C.R.E. 56th DIVISION.	9 R.M.
"	4.8.17		2nd LIEUT. D.S. COUSINS & No.4 SECTION rejoin Company from NORTBECOURT.	9 R.M.
"	5.8.17		CAPT. E.L. MARTIN. M.C. L⁺ D.E. CLERK & 2nd LT. J. ROBERTSON / Transport proceed to NOORDPEENE arriving 10. 0 AM into Billets.	9 R.M.
NOORDPEENE	6.8.17		Transport under CAPT. E.L. MARTIN. M.C. move to STEENVOORDE. E arriving 4. 0 AM about 7. 30 PM 2nd LIEUT. P.L. JAMES & 16 Cyclists arrived from ABEELE having entrained at WATTEN & midnight. LIEUT. J.A. MERCER 2nd LIEUT. V.L. FARFAN & remainder of Company arrived from ABEELE having entrained at WATTEN.	9 R.M.
STEENVOORDE EAST	7.8.17		MAJOR F.G.P. GEDGE rejoined from leave in PARIS & resumed Command of the Company.	Zylu. J.A. Mercer
"	12.8.17		2nd LIEUT. D.S. COUSINS proceeds on leave to ENGLAND.	Zylu.

T1134. Wt. W708—776. 500000. 4/15. Sir J. C. & S.

WAR DIARY
of
INTELLIGENCE SUMMARY.
(Erase heading not required.)

Army Form C. 2118.

512th (London) Field C.R.E.

Instructions regarding War Diaries and Intelligence Summaries are contained in F. S. Regs., Part II. and the Staff Manual respectively. Title pages will be prepared in manuscript.

Place	Date	Hour	Summary of Events and Information	Remarks and references to Appendices
STEENVOORDE EAST	13/8/17		Company move by road to NEW DICKEBUSCH CAMP. MAP REF. SHEET 28 N.N. 1/20.000 H.33 a. 3.3 arriving to join.	John.
NEW DICKEBUSCH CAMP	13/8/17		LIEUT. J.A. MERCER & Nos 1 & 2 SECTIONS employed on improving tracks at I.17 c.7.4 to I.17 a.4.5 & I.7.23 a.7.6. MAP REF. SHEET 28 N.N.	J.M.
"	15/8/17		MAJOR. F.G.P. GEDGE, Headquarters & 4 Section move to SEGARD CHATEAU. MAP REF. SHEET 28 N.Y. H.30. a. 9.2.	J.M.
SEGARD CHATEAU	16/8/17		LIEUT. D.E. CLERK & No 3 & 4 SECTIONS ordered to consolidate JARGON TRENCH in conjunction with the EDINBURGH FIELD Coy. Owing to late receipt of orders Sections did not arrive at site till daylight had broken before working.	J.M.
	17/8/17		MAJOR F.G.P.GEDGE Headquarters & 4 Section move to BUND MAP REF SHEET 28.NN I.21 A. 2.3 on arrival orders were received to concentrate at SEGARD CHATEAU.	J.M.
	17/8/17		3 LIEUT J. ROBERTSON & No 2 SECTION wire JARGON SWITCH between MAP REF. SHEET 28. N.N. J.B.L. 8s.6s. & J.B.L.8.3.	J.M.
	18/8/17		MAJOR. F.G.P. GEDGE, Headquarters & 4 Section, transport under CAPT. E.L. HARTMAN.C.	

Capt E Gedge

Army Form C. 2118.

WAR DIARY
INTELLIGENCE SUMMARY.
(Erase heading not required.)

512 "(London) Field Co. R.E.

Place	Date	Hour	Summary of Events and Information	Remarks and references to Appendices
"	18/8/17		move to OTTAWA CAMP MAP REF. SHEET 28 N.W. G 24 C.8.5.	J.G.
OTTAWA CAMP			LIEUT. J.H. McCULLOCH. R.E. attached to Unit reports for duty.	J.G.
"	20/8/17		Company move by road to II CORPS R.E. PARK MAP REF. SHEET 28 N.W. G.21.K.5.5. under orders of C.R.E. 56 Division & came under orders of C.E.II Corps.	J.G.
BUSSEBOOM	21/8/17		MAJOR F.G.P. GEDGE evacuated to Field Ambulance & CAPT. E.L. MARTIN. M.C. takes over command of the Company.	J.G.
"	25/8/17		Transport under CAPT. E.L. MARTIN. M.C. moved by road to NORDPEENE arriving 7 o'clock pm into Billets.	J.G.
NORDPEENE	26/8/17		Transport under CAPT E.L. MARTIN. M.C. moved by road to BLEUE MAISON arriving 4 o'clock into Billets.	J.G.
"	26/8/17		SAPPERS under LIEUT. J.A. MERCER moved by train from ABEELE to BLEUE MAISON arriving 7 o'clock pm.	J.G.
BLEUE MAISON	26/8/17		LIEUT. D.S. COUSINS rejoins Company from leave in U.K.	J.G.
			MAJOR. F.G.P. GEDGE rejoined from Field Ambulance & resumed Command of the Company on the 27th.	J.G.

J.G. Gedge

Army Form C. 2118.

WAR DIARY
INTELLIGENCE SUMMARY.
(Erase heading not required.)

512th (London) Field 626.

Instructions regarding War Diaries and Intelligence
Summaries are contained in F.S. Regs., Part II.
and the Staff Manual respectively. Title pages
will be prepared in manuscript.

Place	Date	Hour	Summary of Events and Information	Remarks and references to Appendices
BLEUE MAISON	30/5/[?]		Company march to ARQUES, entraining here for BAPAUME WEST, arriving at 11.6.P.M. march to BEAULENCOURT & are in hut.	

MAJOR R. E.
OC 512th (LONDON) FIELD COY. R.E.

T2134. Wt. W708—776. 500000. 4/15. Sir J. C. & S.

Army Form C. 2118.

WAR DIARY
INTELLIGENCE SUMMARY.
(Erase heading not required.)

512th (London) Field C.R.E.

Vol 20

Instructions regarding War Diaries and Intelligence Summaries are contained in F. S. Regs., Part II. and the Staff Manual respectively. Title pages will be prepared in manuscript.

Place	Date	Hour	Summary of Events and Information	Remarks and references to Appendices
BEAULENCOURT	2/9/17		Lieuts. J.A. MERCER & D.E. CLERK report to 56th Field C.R.E. to take over work in hand.	Feb.
"	4/9/17		Company move by road to LEBUCQUIERE arriving 2.30pm. Take over work from 56th Field C.R.E. at 8 pm. Lieuts J A MERCER, D.E. CLERK & 2/Lieuts D.S. COUSINS, V.L. FARFAN – Nos 3 & 4 sections move to advanced billets at MAP REF SHEET 57 c N.W. C.29.a.1.4.	Feb. Feb.
LEBUCQUIERE	7/9/17		Capt. E.L. MARTIN M.C. proceeds to England on leave.	Feb.
"	8/9/17		Lieut. D.E. CLERK & No 4 section rejoin Headquarters & are relieved by Lieut. J.H. McCULLOCH & No 1 & 2 sections who move to advanced billets.	Feb.
"	16.9.17		2/Lieut D.S. COUSINS & No 3 section rejoin Headquarters & are relieved by 2/Lieut. P.L. JAMES & No 4 section who move to advanced billets.	Feb.
"	19.9.17		Capt. E.L. MARTIN M.C. rejoins from leave in England.	Feb.
"	20.9.17		Draft 3 O.R. arrived from R.E. Base Depot.	Feb.
"	23.9.17		No 2 section rejoin Headquarters & are relieved by No 3 section who proceed to advanced billets.	Feb.
"	27.9.17		Lieut. J.H. McCULLOCH proceeds to England on leave.	Feb.

Army Form C. 2118.

WAR DIARY
INTELLIGENCE SUMMARY

512th (London) Field Coy. R.E.

(Erase heading not required.)

Place	Date	Hour	Summary of Events and Information	Remarks and references to Appendices
LEBUCQUIERE	20.9.17		Capt. E.L. Martin M.C. leaves for Veterinary course at No. 7 Veterinary Hospital FORGES LES EAUX.	J.C.
"	30.9.17		Lieut. T.A. Mercer & No. 1 Section rejoin Headquarters & are relieved by No. 2 Section who proceed to advanced billets.	J.C.

J. Crisp
MAJOR R.E.
O/C 512th (LONDON) FIELD COY. R.E.

WAR DIARY
INTELLIGENCE SUMMARY.
(Erase heading not required.)

512 (London) Field Coy. R.E.

Army Form C. 2118.

Place	Date	Hour	Summary of Events and Information	Remarks and references to Appendices
LEBUCQUIERE	2.6.17		The promotion of Lieut. D.S. COUSINS, J. ROBERTSON and V.L. FARFAN has been approved in accordance with G.R.O. 2572 and the badges of Lieutenant may be worn. No.4 Section rejoin H.Q. & are relieved by No.1 Section who proceed to advanced billets.	appx
"	3.6.17		LIEUT. J. ROBERTSON proceeds on leave to England.	appx
"	8.6.17		CAPT. E.L. MARTIN, M.C. rejoins from No.1 VETERINARY HOSPITAL.	appx
"	14.6.17		No.3 Section rejoin H.Q. and are relieved by No.4 Section who proceed to advanced billet.	appx
"	14.6.17		MAJOR F.P. GEDGE proceeds on special leave to England for 1 month and CAPT. E.L. MARTIN, M.C. assumes Command of the Company. LT. COL. E.N. MOZLEY, D.S.O inspects the Company H.Q. on taking over duties as C.R.E. 56th Division.	appx
"	17.6.17		No 2 SECTION rejoin H.Q & are relieved by No. 3 SECTION who proceed to advanced billets.	appx
"	21.6.17		2/LIEUTENANT, T/MAJOR F.G.P. GEDGE promoted LIEUTENANT from 1st JUNE 1916 London Gazette. Oct. 22/17.	appx

E. L. Martin CAPTAIN R.E.
512th (LONDON) FIELD COY. R.E.

Army Form C. 2118.

WAR DIARY
or
INTELLIGENCE SUMMARY.
(Erase heading not required.) 512th (London) Field Coy RE

Instructions regarding War Diaries and Intelligence Summaries are contained in F. S. Regs., Part II. and the Staff Manual respectively. Title pages will be prepared in manuscript.

Place	Date	Hour	Summary of Events and Information	Remarks and references to Appendices
LEBUCQUIERE	22.10.17		LIEUT. T. ROBERTSON rejoins from leave in England.	Appx
"	23.10.17		2 LIEUT. P.L. JAMES rejoins Company H.Q.	Appx
"	25.10.17		LIEUT. V.L. FARFAN proceeds on leave to England.	Appx
"	27.10.17		2 LIEUT. P.L. JAMES evacuated to hospital sick.	Appx
"	28.10.17		No 1 Section rejoin H.Q. and are relieved by No 2 Section who proceed to advanced billets.	Appx
"	30.10.17		The Company's transport inspected by the A.D.V.S. IV Corps.	Appx

S. Ruxton CAPTAIN R.E.
O/c 512TH (LONDON) FIELD COY. R.E.

512TH (LONDON) FIELD COY. R.E.
No ....
Date 31.10.17

WAR DIARY
INTELLIGENCE SUMMARY

Army Form C. 2118.

512th (London) Field C.R.E.

Vol 22

Place	Date	Hour	Summary of Events and Information	Remarks and references to Appendices
LEBUCQUIERE	2.11.17		LIEUT. D.E. CLERK proceeds on leave to England.	
"	3. "		CAPT. E.L. MARTIN M.C. & LIEUT. J.A. MERCER promoted to LIEUTENANTS with precedence from 1/6/1916. London Gazette 30/10/17	
"	"		Sections including Advanced H.Q. are engaged in Raising Steam Brigade C.E.	
"	"		LIEUT. V.L. FABIAN returns from leave in England.	
"	"		LIEUT. M.L. JAMES proceeds to England for Engineer Course.	
"	"		LIEUT. H.R. LESLIE, 15th LONDON REGIMENT, attached to Unit, reports for duty.	
"	14. "		2 Officers & 33 O.R. 168th INFANTRY BRIGADE, attached to Unit, report for duty.	
"	"		4 Sections moved to Advanced Billet.	
"	16. "		1 Officer & 11 O.R. 7th LONDON REGT. attached to Unit & report for duty.	
"	17. "		MAJOR F.R. GEDGE returns upon leave in England & resumed Command of Company.	
"	18. "		CAPT. E.L. MARTIN M.C. moves to Advanced H.Q. for forthcoming operation.	
"	19. "		LIEUT. DE CLERK returns from leave in England & moves to Advanced H.Q.	
"	16,17,18,19&20."		No.1, 2, 3, & 4 Sections were employed on the BEUGNY-BOURSIES Road under CAPTAIN E.L. MARTIN M.C.	
"	18.11.17		LIEUT. J.A. MERCER & No.1 SECTION moved into Billets at MORCHIES.	
"	20.11.17	At 6 A.M.	LIEUT. J.A. MERCER & No.1 SECTION came under orders of 168th Infantry Brigade.	
"	20.11.17	9 A.M.	I sent forward LIEUT DE CLERK R.E. CAPT. TOLIFFE & CAPT. HERRON of the CHESHIRES to reconnoitre CAMBRAI ROAD up to CANAL. At same time LIEUT. SIKES R.E. & 2 PLATOONS "B" Company CHESHIRES went forward to clear ArB obstruction. Reports in at 6.30 a.m. 21/11/17 that Horse Transport could go up to "C" but not past, and also road report from LIEUT CLERK. Copy of which I sent to C.R.E. 7.30 am & 168th BRIGADE who ordered road to be cleared. 7 I.H. 9 ami received report that 1 Platoon CHESHIRES were working on shell holes at front line.	attached Sketch Nos marked "A"

[signature] MAJOR R.E.
O/C 512th (LONDON) FIELD COY. R.E.

D. D. & L., London, E.C.
(A8004) Wt. W1771/M2-31 750,000 5/17 Sch 52 Forms/C.2118/14

Army Form C. 2118.

WAR DIARY
or
INTELLIGENCE SUMMARY.
(Erase heading not required.)

512th (London) Field C.R.E.

Place	Date	Hour	Summary of Events and Information	Remarks and references to Appendices
	21/11/17		At 9.30 am rode up to BOURSIES & then reconnoitred road up to CANAL. At 8.0 pm I sent forward "A" C Company CHESHIRES to commence deviation at CRATERS D+E & 35 wagons carrying material. 1 section #16 (Edinburgh) Field C.R.E. under LIEUT. BILES & 1 section 518th (London) Field Co. R.E. under LIEUT. PINNOCH were employed during nights of 21/22 & 22/23 on placing across Bridges over benches last rivet of both Craters. Detached parties of the same sections continued spiking down & maintaining the corduroy track on 23rd, 24th. When they were relieved by LIEUT. DECLERG & No.3 Section 512th (London) Field C.R.E. with attached Infantry. Deviation D was corduroyed at 5.0am 24th. At 5.0am I sent forward H.Q. Sapper & some CHESHIRES to spike down corduroy laid during night.	
	21/11.	Night	No. 1 Section under LIEUT. T.A. MERCER were employed in clearing roads & tracks on the LUVERVAL INCHY Road over "no mans land".	
	22.11.17	At 5.30 pm	I sent forward parties of "A.B.C.&D" Company CHESHIRES (with 35 wagons of trans & 20 wagons D.A.C. under CAPT. BOYS) to complete deviation at D+E. At 7.0 pm an Officer under CAPT. GLENDENNING returned to BOURSIES with 2 horses CHESHIRES & 9 loaded Wagons having received orders from Q.V.R. that enemy was counter attacking in force. I sent 1 out 1 Platoon to north of BOURSIES to form defensive flank, until I could get further information. At 7.30 pm CAPT. GLENDENNING came back from CRATER AT[?] and exhibit went out gave orders to CAPT. GLENDENNING to return with transport to the CRATERS to know out covering parts if necessary. At 9.0 pm transport Officer CAPT. BOYS reported to me that he was unable to close CRATER D as corduroy was slipping. Oo proceeded to site & had same hindered with rails. First wagon arrived CRATER! D & at 9.0 pm offloaded at Western end of CRATER. E. I organised work at E laid single track corduroy & passing first Bridging wagon over at 11.0 pm.	

Major R. E.
O/C 512th (LONDON) FIELD COY. R.E.

War Diary

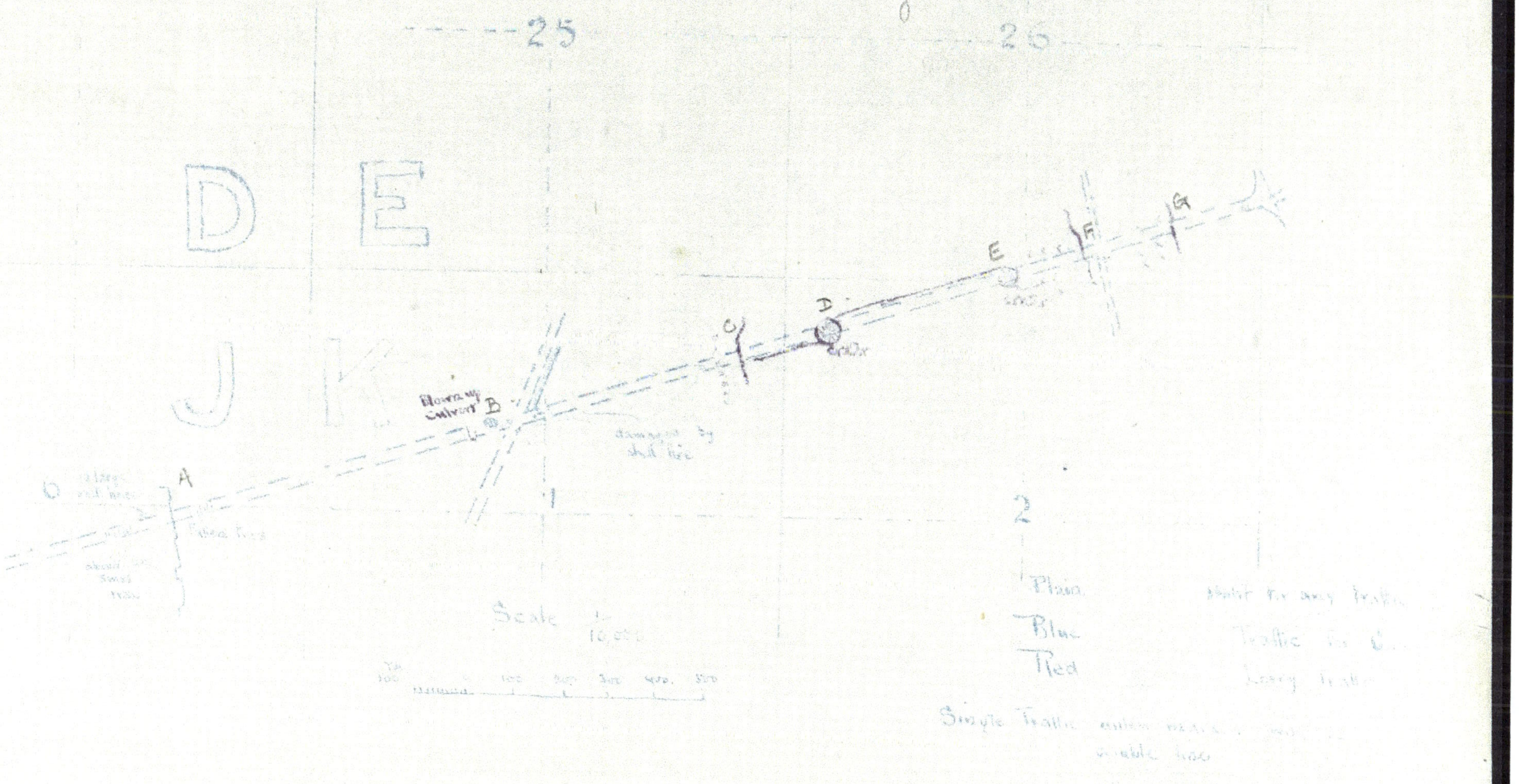
25
26
D
E
J
K
A
Blown up culvert B
damaged by shell fire
C
D
E
F
G
1
2
Scale 1/10,000
Plain
Blue
Red

Army Form C. 2118.

WAR DIARY
or
INTELLIGENCE SUMMARY.
(Erase heading not required.)

512th (London) Field Coy R.E.

Instructions regarding War Diaries and Intelligence Summaries are contained in F. S. Regs., Part II. and the Staff Manual respectively. Title pages will be prepared in manuscript.

Place	Date	Hour	Summary of Events and Information	Remarks and references to Appendices
			7/416 Edw Field Coy	
			MAJOR. PARKS Bridging Wagons having arrived about 10.30pm. I passed the last obstruction at 12.o'clock midnight they all arrived afew minutes later at the CANAL.	
	22/23	Night	LIEUT. J.A. MERCER & No 1 SECTION continued clearing roads tracks etc.	
	23/24		CAPT E.L. MARTIN M.C. & 3 Sections Sappers here given orders to commence widening road at the eastern end of BOURSIES with attached Infantry. They returned to Billets at LAGNICOURT at 4.0pm 24th having marched 11 miles worked 10 hours on road, & marched back to LAGNICOURT.	
	23/24		LIEUT. J.A. MERCER & No 1 SECTION continued clearing road & other men C.T. across no mans land which was commenced by "C" Company CHESHIRES.	
	24. 11 C.		At 3.0pm orders were received sent to CAPT. E.L. MARTIN. M.C. for himself + 3 sections Sappers to move to BOURSIES & dig in & proceeded to BOURSIES at 5.0pm + explained nature of work to sections No 2 & 4 worked at CRATERS whole night of 24/25th from the 24/25th. I had at my disposal for improving work already done the following troops. 5/5 A Troops E.R.E. 142nd Labour Co. Some 24th entrade. LIEUT DE CLERK & No 3 SECTION undertook maintenance of deviation during daylight hours. At midday 25th I ordered LIEUT DE CLERK & No 3 SECTION to move forward to D & E CRATERS to dig themselves in & remain as personel maintenance party.	
	24/25	Night	LIEUT. A.R. LESLIE & No 1 SECTION employed making 3 places for LONDON SCOTTISH in HINDENSBURG LINE.	

G.J. Mills MAJOR R.E.
O/C 512th (LONDON) FIELD COY. R.E.

Army Form C. 2118.

WAR DIARY
or
INTELLIGENCE SUMMARY. 512th (London) Field C.R.E.
(Erase heading not required.)

Place	Date	Hour	Summary of Events and Information	Remarks and references to Appendices
	24 h.m. 25/4		LIEUT. J. ROBERTSON rejoined Headquarters sick.	
	25/4	Night	LIEUT A.R. LESLIE & No 1 SECTION employed making 2 Blocks for the RANGERS on the HINDENBURG LINE.	
	"	"	2 Sections worked on widening corduroy at CRATERS DYE all night	
	26/4		At 8.30 am C.R.E. telephoned orders that Company came under orders of G.O.C. 168th Brigade	
			Ordered LIEUT J.A. MERCER to move No1 SECTION to dig in at BOURRIES. LIEUT J.A. MERCER &	
			LIEUT A.R. LESLIE returning to H.Q. LEBUCQUIERE.	
			During above mentioned period 1 Driver & Horse were under orders of S.A.S. D.A.C. for	
			transportation & suffered casualties. 3 Drivers wounded & 3 Horse killed & 2 wounded.	
	26/4	Night	4 Sections engaged digging PICCADILLY forming ADV DUMP	
	27/28	"	4 Sections sappers engaged sewing storm truce.	
	28/30	"	4 Sections sappers continue wiring.	
	29/30	"	4 Sections sappers complete wiring & strengthen bridge over old front line.	
	"		Attached infantry report back to 168 Brigade	
	30/4		Headquarters & Transport under Major J.G.P. Sedge move to FREMICOURT arriving 11.0pm	

J.G. Sedge MAJOR R. E.
O/C 512th (LONDON) FIELD COY. R.E.

Army Form C. 2118.

WAR DIARY
OR
INTELLIGENCE SUMMARY.

512th (London) Field Coy. R.E.

(Erase heading not required)

Instructions regarding War Diaries and Intelligence Summaries are contained in F.S. Regs., Part II. and the Staff Manual respectively. Title pages will be prepared in manuscript.

Place	Date	Hour	Summary of Events and Information	Remarks and references to Appendices
FREMICOURT	1/5/17 Night		Nos 1, 3 & 4 Sections employed in digging 8 Strong Points. Headquarters & Transport under Major F.G.P. GEDGE moved by road to BEAUMENCOURT arriving 11am into huts. No 2 Section join Headquarters from BOCKSIES arriving 9.30am. Hospital a/Lieut. G.H.F. MADDISON awarded the MILITARY MEDAL for an act of gallantry in the field.	
	2/5/17		Major H.O.R. arrived from R.E. Base Depot. Nos 1,2, & 4 Sections under LIEUT. DE CLERQ move by road to FREMICOURT & entrain line for	
BEAUMENCOURT	3/5/17		BEAUQUESNE, RIVIERE & march to SIMENCOURT arriving 5.0am. Headquarters & Transport under MAJOR F.G.P. GEDGE move by road to SIMENCOURT arriving 6.45am into huts. CAPT. E.L. MARTIN. M.C. proceeds to take over command of 128th Field R.E.	
SIMENCOURT	4/5/17		LIEUT. R.A. MERCER proceeds on leave to England. Sergeant ERWIN TUCKER. H. awarded the MILITARY MEDAL for an act of gallantry in the field. No. 54645 Lance CROUCHMAN A. awarded the MILITARY MEDAL. Company move by road to ECOIVRES arriving 3.0pm into Billets.	
	5/5/17		LIEUTS. F. ROBERTSON & Lt. FARFAN. proceed to LOURIE, take over work from 20th Field R.E. Company move by road to ECURIE arriving 13.30pm into huts & No 4 Section & LIEUT. ROBERTSON & D.S. COUSINS proceed to advanced billets at map ref. Sheet 51NW. B 21. a. 6. 9.	
ECURIE	6/5/17 Night		Nos. 4 Sections employed wiring RED LINE.	
	7/5/17		4 Sections Sappers continue wiring.	
	8/5/17		4 Sections Sappers continue wiring. and Supers AT. Line	

[signature] MAJOR R.E.
O/C 512th (LONDON) FIELD COY. R.E.

56

2/1 London 1ᵈ Coy
R.E.

Vol II

Army Form C. 2118.

WAR DIARY
or
INTELLIGENCE SUMMARY.

(Erase heading not required.)

512th (London) Field Co. R.E.

Instructions regarding War Diaries and Intelligence Summaries are contained in F.S. Regs, Part II. and the Staff Manual respectively. Title pages will be prepared in manuscript.

Place	Date	Hour	Summary of Events and Information	Remarks and references to Appendices
ECURIE	10/11		Draft 3 O.R. from R.E. Base Depot.	
"	11/12	NIGHT	Lieut. A.R. LESLIE moved to Advanced Relief & Lieut. D.E. COUSINS rejoined Headquarters.	
"			3 sections sappers continued mining. SUPPORT LINE	
"	12	DAY	Draft 2 O.R. arrived from R.E. Base Depot.	
"	12/13	NIGHT	3 sections sappers continue mining.	
"	14		Major H.G.P. Godge leaves for R.E. Base, ROUEN & Lieut. D.E. CLERK assumes command of the Company	
"	14/15	NIGHT	3 sections sappers continue mining.	
"	16		Draft 1 O.R. arrived from R.E. Base Depot.	
"	16/17	NIGHT	3 sections sappers continue mining.	
"	17		Lieut. V.L. FARFAN & No.3 section joins Unit for duty & assumes temporary command of Company	
"			Map Ref. B.10 c.1.0.	
"	18		Capt. J.T.F. HENDERSON, M.C. joins Unit for duty & assumes temporary command of Company	
"	17/18	NIGHT	2 sections sappers continue mining	
"	18		Lieut. V.L. FARFAN & No.3 section rejoin Headquarters.	
"	18/19		2 sections sappers continue mining	
"	20		Lieut. V.L. FARFAN absorbed Divisional Mining Officer and attached to C.R.E. 56th Division	
"			Lieut. J.A. MERCER rejoins from leave in England.	
"			Headquarters & No.1 & 2 sections under Capt. J.T.F. HENDERSON, M.C. move to St CATHERINE	
"			arriving 10 o'clock into Huts.	
"	21		Draft of 2 O.R. arrive from R.E. Base Depot.	
St CATHERINE	21			

Signature: Major R.E.
O/C 512th (LONDON) FIELD COY. R.E.

Army Form C. 2118.

WAR DIARY
or
INTELLIGENCE SUMMARY.

512/(London) Field Co. R.E.

(Erase heading not required.)

Instructions regarding War Diaries and Intelligence Summaries are contained in F. S. Regs., Part II. and the Staff Manual respectively. Title pages will be prepared in manuscript.

Place	Date	Hour	Summary of Events and Information	Remarks and references to Appendices
ST CATHERINE	21.9.17		Nos 2 & 4 SECTIONS rejoin Headquarters.	
"	22 "		Nos 1 & 3 SECTIONS move forward & dig in at RAILWAY CUTTING. S.26.d.4.4.	
"	23 "		CAPT. J.T.F. HENDERSON M.C. takes over command of the Company & wears the badges of MAJOR.	
"	"		The promotion of LIEUT. E.A. MERCER has been approved and he wears the badges of CAPTAIN in a/c to town.	
"	24 "		LIEUT. D.E. CLERK, 2/LIEUT. A.R. LESLIE & No4 SECTION move forward who in at RAILWAY CUTTING	
"	26 "		LIEUT. D.S. COUSINS proceeds on leave to England.	
"	28 "		LIEUT. Z. ROBERTSON moves forward to Advanced H.Q. at RAILWAY CUTTING.	

[signature]
O/C 512th (LONDON) FIELD COY. R.E.   MAJOR R. E.

Army Form C. 2118.

WAR DIARY
or
INTELLIGENCE-SUMMARY.
(Erase heading not required.)

512 (London) Field C.E.

Instructions regarding War Diaries and Intelligence Summaries are contained in F.S. Regs., Part II. and the Staff Manual respectively. Title pages will be prepared in manuscript.

Place	Date	Hour	Summary of Events and Information	Remarks and references to Appendices
ST. CATHERINE	1.1.18		Draft 3 O.R. arrived from R.E. Base.	
"	5.1.18		No1 Section, Headquarters & first transport under Capt. J.A. MERCER move to ROBERTS CAMP A.24.c.4.2. & remainder of transport move to ECOIVRES. Nos 2, 3 & 4 SECTIONS under LIEUT. D.E. CLERK move to ROBERTS CAMP, arriving 11.30 a.m. into hut.	
ROBERTS CAMP.	13.1.18		LIEUT. D.S. COUSINS returns from leave in England.	
"	18.1.18		LIEUT. D.E. CLERK proceeds to TINCQUES & is attached to Divisional H.Q. as R.E. Supply Officer.	
"	23.1.18		LIEUT. J. ROBERTSON proceeds on leave to U.K.	
"			During period from 19/31st the Company were engaged on revetting the battery trench & erecting machine gun emplacements from MAP REF. (sheet 51-B-N.W.) H.I.C.3.3. to A.12.d.1.9.	

[signature] MAJOR R.E.
O/C 512th (LONDON) FIELD COY. R.E.

WAR DIARY
or
INTELLIGENCE SUMMARY.
(Erase heading not required.)

Army Form C. 2118.

5712 YA C. Pl. JA 25

Instructions regarding War Diaries and Intelligence Summaries are contained in F.S. Regs., Part II. and the Staff Manual respectively. Title pages will be prepared in manuscript.

Place	Date	Hour	Summary of Events and Information	Remarks and references to Appendices
ROBERTS	25/1/18		CAPT. J.A. MERCER joins headquarters from ECOIVRES	
CAMP	6.1.18		MAJOR T.T.F. HENDERSON. M.C. reports to H&O Q'ld Coy. R.E. to take over command.	
"	11.1.18		MAJOR T.T.F. HENDERSON. M.C. proceeds to R.E. SCHOOL, BLENDECQUES for course. T	
"	12.2.18		CAPT. J.A. MERCER assumed Command of Company.	
			Headquarters, transport & No 1 Section under LIEUT V.L. FAREAN move to ST CATHERINE	
			on billets & remainder of Company under CAPT. J.A. MERCER move to CUTTING	
			MAP REF. 3.h. d.4.9. with Kellers Bivouacs	
			Staff & C.R.E. arrived from R.E. Base	
			LIEUT D.E. CLEAR rejoined from DIV H.Q.	
SCATHERNE			LIEUT D.E. CLEAR moved forward to billets in CUTTING.	
"	8.2.18		LIEUT J. ROBERTSON rejoins from leave in England	
			No 4 SECTION move forward to billets in CUTTING	
"	9.2.18		LIEUT J. ROBERTSON move forward to billets in CUTTING	
"	14.2.18		LIEUT A.K. LESLIE rejoins his Section	
"	22.2.18		Draft of 28 OR arrive from R.E. Base	

Army Form C. 2118.

WAR DIARY
or
INTELLIGENCE SUMMARY.
(Erase heading not required.)

Place	Date	Hour	Summary of Events and Information	Remarks and references to Appendices
SCATHERINE	31.3.18		No forward billets shelled during the afternoon. The Company had 8 casualties as result. During period from 11th to 28th the Company were engaged as follows:- 2 sections on Corps reserve, 1 section on dugouts in Brigade Area. 1 section on dugouts in NORTH TYNE ALLEY D.22.d.9.9.	AAA BBB

[signature] CAPTAIN R.E.
512th (LONDON) FIELD COY. R.E.

56th Div.

WAR DIARY

512th (LONDON) FIELD COMPANY, R.E.

M A R C H

1 9 1 8

Army Form C. 2118.

WAR DIARY
or
INTELLIGENCE SUMMARY

(Erase heading not required.)

512th (London) Field C.R.E.

Instructions regarding War Diaries and Intelligence Summaries are contained in F. S. Regs., Part II. and the Staff Manual respectively. Title pages will be prepared in manuscript.

Hour, Date, Place	Summary of Events and Information	Remarks and references to Appendices
ST. CATHERINE. 1.3.1918	MAJOR. J.T.F. HENDERSON. M.C. returns from R.E. School BLENDECQUES & resumed Command of the Company	W/St 26
" 2	MAJOR J.T.F. HENDERSON. M.C. moves to Forward H.Q. in the Cutting.	
" 3	CAPT. J.A. MERCER joins near H.Q.	
" 4	LT. V.L. FARFAN moves to Forward billets in the Cutting.	
" 9	1 draft 1 O.R. arrives from R.E. Base Depot.	
" 15	LT. D.S. COUSINS joins near H.Q. sick Gas N.Y.D.	
" 17	LT. V.L. FARFAN joins near H.Q.	
" 18	CAPT. J.A. MERCER moves to Forward billets in the Cutting.	
" 19	LT. V.L. FARFAN proceeds on leave to England.	
" 21	1 draft 1 O.R. arrives from R.E. Base Depot.	
" 21	2/Lt A.R. LESLIE 15th London Regt. attached to Unit reports for duty.	
" 24	1 draft 5 OR' arrives from R.E. Base Depot.	
" 27	LT. D.S. COUSINS evacuated to C.C.S.	
" 28	At 4.30 A.M MAJOR J.T.F. HENDERSON. M.C. reported to left Brigade H.Q. and received orders for Company to occupy GREEN LINE North of RAILWAY POST. 10.30 AM Orders were received from C.R.E. for Company to withdraw from GREEN LINE to JUNCTION REDOUBT, and R.E. Battalion was formed consisting of 3 Divisional Field Co's R.E. & 1 Tunnelling Co.	

Army Form C. 2118.

WAR DIARY
or
INTELLIGENCE SUMMARY. 512 London Field C.R.E.
(Erase heading not required.)

Place	Date	Hour	Summary of Events and Information	Remarks and references to Appendices
			and MAJOR J.T.F. HENDERSON. M.C. to be in temporary command of the R.E. Battalion for combatant duties but not for normal R.E. work. The 176' Tunnelling Coy. R.E. being lent to the Right Brigade. H.Q. Coln 416' Field C.R.E. moved from JUNCTION REDOUBT to BLANCHE POST and garrisoned that post. H.Q. Coln 513' Field C.R.E. moved from JUNCTION REDOUBT to TONGUE POST and garrisoned that post. H.Q. Coln 512' Field C.R.E. & 416' Field C.R.E. evacuated their posts to go forward and form blocks in C.T.'s & strengthen RED LINE. Canadian Engineers were informed by 512' Field C.R.E. of evacuation of JUNCTION REDOUBT. 416' Field C.R.E. did not evacuate their post until relieved by share personnel of 'B' Reserve Brigade who garrisoned BLANCHE POST. 512' Field C.R.E. & 416' Field C.R.E. returned to their posts (i.e. JUNCTION REDOUBT & BLANCHE POST) on completion of tasks & garrisoned them. H. Q.O. this orders were received that the Battalion would be relieved on relief 512' Field C.R.E. withdraw to PLYMOUTH CAMP, 513' Field C.R.E. to HARDY CAMP, 416' Field C.R.E. to EDINBURGH CAMP. Companies arriving at camps about H. 0 AM. on 30th when the Companies of the Battalion became under the direct orders of the C.R.E. MAJOR. J.T.F. HENDERSON. M.C. resumed command of 512' Field C.R.E.	
	30.3.18		At 5 a.m. the 176' Tunnelling Coy R.E. ceased to be under Command of 56' Division	

Army Form C. 2118.

WAR DIARY
or
INTELLIGENCE SUMMARY.   512'' (London) Field Co R.E.
(Erase heading not required.)

Instructions regarding War Diaries and Intelligence Summaries are contained in F. S. Regs., Part II. and the Staff Manual respectively. Title pages will be prepared in manuscript.

Place	Date	Hour	Summary of Events and Information	Remarks and references to Appendices
	30.3.18		512'' Field C.R.E. (less transport & H.Q.) moved to ANZIN into Billets arriving at 12' noon. H.Q & Transport joined Company at ANZIN at 3.0 pm.	
	31.		Company commenced training. During period 11.2.18 to 31.3.18 Company sustained casualties:- Died of wounds 1. Wounded 38.	

Signature
MAJOR R. E.
O/C 512th (LONDON) FIELD COY. R.E.

56th Divisional Engineers

512th
~~516~~ (London) FIELD COMPANY R. E.

APRIL 1918.

WAR DIARY
or
INTELLIGENCE SUMMARY — 512th London Field R.E.
(Erase heading not required.)

Army Form C. 2118.

Hour, Date, Place		Summary of Events and Information	Remarks and references to Appendices
ANZIN.	April 1/14	Company employed training	
"	5th	Company move by road to ESTREE COUCHIE arriving 1.30 pm into Billets	
ESTREE COUCHIE	6th	Company move by road to AGNEZ LES DUISANS arriving 5.0 pm into Billets	
AGNEZ LES DUISANS	7th	Headquarters + transport under Capt. J.A. MERCER move to BERNEVILLE into Billets + 4 sections + others under Major. J.T.F. HENDERSON M.C move to RONVILLE CAVES.	
BERNEVILLE.	"	2/Lieut. J. HENWOOD joined Company from R.E. Base. Reinforcement.	
"	"	405464th Sergt. W.E. DALLENGER + No 546391 A/2/Corpl H.T. DYE awarded the MILITARY MEDAL.	
"	8th	2/Lt V.L FARFAN rejoins from leave in U.K + proceeds to forward H.Q.	
"	"	(a) RONVILLE CAVES with 2/Lieut. J. HENWOOD	
"	13th	1 N.C.O.R arrive from R.E. Base Depot.	
"	17th	Lt. J. ROBERTSON to Hospital Wounded (Shell Gas)	
"	20th	Lt. V.L FARFAN joins Rear H.Q.	
"	23rd	Draft 21 O.R arrive from R.E. Base Depot. + Capt. J.A. MERCER goes forward	
"	26th	Draft No 21/3 sections under Major J.T.F. HENDERSON M.C forward H.Q. + move to ARRAS.	
"	27th	2/Lt V.L FARFAN to Hospital sick + Lt. J. ROBERTSON rejoins from hospital	
"	30th	No 1 Section under Lt. DE CLERK join forward H.Q. in ARRAS	
"	"	Period "16.30" Work of Company	
"	"	RONVILLE CAVES demolition.	
"	"	Dugout Work	
"	"	Defence line work.	

H. Henderson
Major R.E.
O.C. 512 London Field Company R.E.

Army Form C. 2118.

WAR DIARY
or
INTELLIGENCE SUMMARY
(Erase heading not required.)

Instructions regarding War Diaries and Intelligence Summaries are contained in F.S. Regs., Part II. and the Staff Manual respectively. Title pages will be prepared in manuscript.

512 (London) Field C.R.E.

Hour, Date, Place	Summary of Events and Information	Remarks and references to Appendices
5.5.18 BERNEVILLE	Lt E.R.A.TOODY 47 "Labour Coy" attached to Unit reports for duty	
8 "	Draft 15 O.R. arrive from R.E. Base Depot.	
10 "	Lt. D.E.CLERK O/c No. 4 Q. & Lt. J. ROBERTSON moves to forward	
12 "	Billets in ARRAS shelled. 2 casualties.	
13 "	Draft 2 O.R. arrive from R.E. Base Depot	
17 "	" 3 " " " "	
21 "	" 1 " " " "	
22 "	" 4 " " " "	
25 "	" 1 " " " "	
26 "	" 1 " " " "	
	Company transport inspected by C.R.E. 56th Division.	
30 "	Lt A.R. LESLIE joins coy from H.Q. & Lt. D.E. CLERK to coy to form A.H.Q.	
	Period 1st to 31st Work of Company. Digging & wiring Jew gitter	
	Strung telegraph burden. Bugout work. Billet improvement Lack areas.	
	Reserve.	

J.H. Henderson
MAJOR R.E.
O/C 512th (LONDON) FIELD COY. R.E.

Army Form C. 2118.

WAR DIARY
or
INTELLIGENCE SUMMARY
(Erase heading not required.)

512TH (LONDON FIELD COY.) R.E.

Vol 2 XA

Hour, Date, Place		Summary of Events and Information	Remarks and references to Appendices
BERNEVILLE	3. 6. 18	LT. N.L. FARFAN & 10. O.R. join from R.E. Base Depot - reinforcement.	
"	4 "	LT. N.L. FARFAN moved to Forward H.Q. in ARRAS.	
"	5 "	MAJOR. J.T.F. HENDERSON M.C. join rear H.Q.	
"	6 "	MAJOR. J.T.F. HENDERSON proceeds on leave to U.K. & CAPT. J.A. MERCER assumes command of the Company.	
"	8 "	1st/Staff. Sgt. O.B. Curtis from R.E. Base Depot, reinforcement	
"	12 "	No. 2 Section from rear H.Q. Journeyed to rest	
"	13 "	No. 2 Section rejoin Forward H.Q.	
"	14 "	PTE. E. R. TOOBY joins 180 M.G. & rejoin Forward H.Q. on 15th	
"	16 "	LT. T. HENWOOD & No. 3 Section join rear H.Q. for rest	
"	"	Draft 15 O.R. arrive from R.E. Base Depot reinforcement	
"	"	2LT. J. HENWOOD & No 3 Section rejoin Forward H.Q.	
"	20 "	LT. DE CLERK & No 1 Section join rear H.Q. for period of rest.	
"	"	rejoin Forward H.Q. on 23rd	
"	23 "	MAJOR J.T.F. HENDERSON M.C. returns from leave in UK resumes Command of the Company.	
"	24 "	MAJOR J.T.F. HENDERSON M.C. moves to Forward H.Q.	
"	"	No 4 Section join rear H.Q. for period of rest	
"	25 "	LT. E.R. TOOBY rejoins Coy HQ on 16th/6/18	
"	"	LT. J. ROBERTSON joins rear H.Q. & LT. A.R. LESLIE rejoins Forward H.Q.	

WAR DIARY
INTELLIGENCE SUMMARY
(Erase heading not required.)

Army Form C. 2118.

512TH (LONDON) FIELD COY. R.E.

Instructions regarding War Diaries and Intelligence Summaries are contained in F.S. Regs, Part II. and the Staff Manual respectively. Title pages will be prepared in manuscript.

Hour, Date, Place		Summary of Events and Information	Remarks and references to Appendices
BERNEVILLE	26.6.18	CAPT T.A. PIERCE joins Coy. Aca. M.O. for rest. Returns forward H.Q. on 20?	ЖЖ ЖЖ
	25	C.R.E. 56th Divn. Orders inspect forward billets.	
	25	33 O.R. in forward billets isolated owing to a case of German Spinal Meningitis.	
		Present at 6.30 p.m. Work of Company.	
		Recent task was, Behind Feuchy trench, for raiding purpose. Living trench bridges.	ЖЖ ЖЖ
		Better improvement track over	
	20	MAJOR J.T.F. HENDERSON M.C reports to C.R.E. to take over duties of acting C.R.E.	ЖЖ ЖЖ
		Major B. McLay Browne N° 654363. a/Coy. Sgt. Maj C.J.W. EGGERSTON	
		Distinguished Conduct Medal. Mention in Dispatches of Capt T.A. PIERCE.	

H. Andulu MAJOR R.E.
O/C 512th (LONDON) FIELD COY. R.E.

WAR DIARY
INTELLIGENCE SUMMARY
(Erase heading not required.)

Army Form C. 2118.

512th (London) Field Coy. R.E.

Place	Hour, Date	Summary of Events and Information	Remarks and references to Appendices
Benneville	12.7.18	Lt. DECLERCK & V.L. FARFAN join near H.Q.	
"	13	CAPT. J.A. MERCER & No 1, 2, 1, 3 Sections move by road to HABARCQ. & Lt. J. ROBERTSON. Sp. & 4 Sections & transport move by road to HABARCQ. Company arriving 4.45pm into Billets.	
HABARCQ	14	Company move by road to HOUVIN HOUVIGNEUL arriving 3.0pm into Billet.	
HOUVIN-H.	15	Company move by road to BEUGIN arriving 4.30pm into Billet.	
BEUGIN	16	MAJOR J.T.F. HENDERSON. M.C. rejoins from C.R.E. & resumed Command of the Company.	
"	18	2/Lieut. A.R. LESLIE proceeds to XVII Corps Lewis Gun school for course.	
"	18	Company move by road to BAZIS arriving 11.0AM into Billet.	
"	19	MAJOR J.T.F. HENDERSON. M.C. to Hospital sick and CAPT. J.A. MERCER assumed Command of the Company.	
"	23	MAJOR J.T.F. HENDERSON. M.C. rejoins from Hospital & resumed Command of the Company. Period 1-12. Company employed on dugouts in Div. Area. Period 17-31. Company training.	

H Henderson
MAJOR R.E.
O/C 512th (LONDON) FIELD COY. R.E.

Army Form C. 2118.

WAR DIARY
or
INTELLIGENCE SUMMARY. 512th (London) Field Coy R.E.

(Erase heading not required.)

Instructions regarding War Diaries and Intelligence Summaries are contained in F.S. Regs., Part II. and the Staff Manual respectively. Title pages will be prepared in manuscript.

512TH (LONDON) FIELD COY., R.E.

Vol 31

Place	Date	Hour	Summary of Events and Information	Remarks and references to Appendices
BAVS	1.5.18		Headquarters & transport under CAPT. T.A.MERCER move by road to BERNEVILLE arriving 3.45am into Billets. Remainder of the Company leave by train for ARRAS detraining at DAINVILLE.	
ARRAS	5.		2/LT AR LESLIE rejoins from XVII Corps Lewis Gun school under to proceed H.Q. in ARRAS	
	6.		1 O.R. reinforcement arrives from R.E. Base Depot	
	15.		LT DE CLARE proceeds on 21 days school leave to U.K.	
	17.		Headquarters & transport under CAPT. T.A.MERCER move by road to AMBRINES arriving 2.30pm into Billets. 4 Sections Sappers under MAJOR. J.T.F HENDERSON. M.C. move to BERNEVILLE arriving 8 oclock pm into Billets.	
AMBRINES	18.		Headquarters & transport under CAPT. T.A. MERCER move by road to SARS LES BOIS arriving 11am. Remainder of Company under MAJOR. J.T.F HENDERSON M.C. move from BERNEVILLE to	
SARS LES BOIS	20.		SARS LES BOIS by Light Railway detraining at LEINCOURT arriving 3.30pm into Billets. Company move by road to GRAND ROULLECOURT arriving 10.30am into Billets.	
GRAND ROULLECOURT	21st		Company move by road to GAUDIEMPRE arriving 12.30am & 2.22 into Billets.	
GAUDIEMPRE	22nd		Company move by road to BLAIREVILLE arriving 7.30 pm into Billets. Coys. 4 Sections Sappers under MAJOR. J.T.F HENDERSON M.C. move to Jerusalem Road	
BLAIREVILLE	23rd		Map Ref. S.W. a. 9.2.	
	24th		Transport under CAPT. T.A. MERCER move to area S. 10 d. 4.3 + bivouac.	
	25th		MAJOR. J.T.F HENDERSON. M.C. LT. F. ROBERTSON. LT. AR LESLIE. 2/Lt I.H. CHARD & 213 sections move to dugouts at T.19. a. 5.3. LT. V.L FARFAN & 7 Sappers depart to BERNEVILLE	

O/C 512th (LONDON) FIELD COY., R.E.

Army Form C. 2118.

WAR DIARY
or
INTELLIGENCE SUMMARY.
(Erase heading not required.)

512th London Field Co. R.E.

Instructions regarding War Diaries and Intelligence Summaries are contained in F. S. Regs., Part II. and the Staff Manual respectively. Title pages will be prepared in manuscript.

512TH LONDON FIELD COY., R.E.

Place	Date	Hour	Summary of Events and Information	Remarks and references to Appendices
	26.8.18		Ateliers	
			for A.A.R.E. work.	
			Forward Section under MAJOR J.T.F. HENDERSON M.C. move to area S.11.c.5.7 v bivouac.	
	27		2 O.Rs reinforcements arrive from R.E. Base Depot	
	28		LT. J. ROBERTSON + 12 O.Rs move to CROISILLES are engaged in searching for BOOBY TRAPS, reconnoitring the HINDENBURG LINE tunnels + caves.	
			5 O.Rs reinforcements arrive from R.E. Base Depot	
	29		Section under MAJOR J.T.F. HENDERSON M.C. move to Area T.22.a.1.8 N of CROISILLES into shelters	
			LT. J. ROBERTSON's party rejoin.	
	31		Section under MAJOR J.T.F. HENDERSON M.C. move to Bivouacs at S.11.c.5.7. v LT. J. ROBERTSON's party rejoin.	
			CAPT. T.A. MERCER proceeds on leave to U.K.	
	Period 1-16		Company employed on dugouts in Divisional Area.	
	23-31		" " Reconnoitring roads, wells, cleaning dugouts	
			Erecting + repairing bridges over the COJEUL RIVER, found not thro' at T.19.d. + T.26.c. Clearing shelters repairing same for Advanced D.H.Q. resecting + repairing NISSEN huts for Div. H.Q.	
			All work references on sheet 51c S.W. Edition 8ᵈ LOCAL	

W. Wallis Esq
MAJOR R.E.
O/C 512ᵗʰ (LONDON) FIELD COY. R.E.

Army Form C. 2118.

WAR DIARY
INTELLIGENCE SUMMARY

(Erase heading not required.)

Instructions regarding War Diaries and Intelligence Summaries are contained in F. S. Regs., Part II. and the Staff Manual respectively. Title pages will be prepared in manuscript.

517 (LONDON) FIELD COY. R.E.

Place	Date	Hour	Summary of Events and Information	Remarks and references to Appendices
	1/9/18		4 Sections Sappers under MAJOR J.T.F. HENDERSON. M.C. move to S.11.c.5.7. & bivouac. Lieut. J. ROBERTSON & party of 12 Sappers rejoin Company from CROISILLES.	
	6th		Company move by road to VIS-EN-ARTOIS, & Sappers proceed to O.9.c.3.3. into Dugouts and Bivouacs, and H.Q.rs. and Transport proceed to O.13.b.2.1.	
	7th		No 1 Section move to P.13.d.6.4. No 2 Section to P.9.d.4.0. No 3 & 4 Sections to O.9.B.9.6.	
	8th		No 4 Section under MAJOR J.T.F. HENDERSON. M.C. move to P.19.a.9.8. into Dugouts and Bivouacs. 2 Lieut A.R. LESLIE reports to 513 (London) Field Company R.E. for duty. Lieut. D.E. Clerk rejoined from leave in U.K.	
	9th		Nos 1 & 2 Sections rejoined forward H.Qrs. at P.19.a.9.8. Lieut D.E.CLERK joins forward H.Qrs.	
	10th		Lieut V.L. FARFAN & 12 Sappers report to Divisional Artillery for R.A.R.E. work. No 3 Section join forward H.Qrs. P.19.a.9.8.	
	15th		Party attached to Divisional Artillery increased to 25 men.	
	17th		Capt I.A. MERCER returns from leave in U.K.	
	18th		Lieut. J. ROBERTSON joins forward H.Qrs.	
	19th		Lieut. D.E. CLERK reports to C.R.E. to take over Adjutants duties.	
	20th		4 Sections Sappers under MAJOR J.T.F. HENDERSON. M.C. move to BLANGY. G.23.B.2.c. late with R.A.R.E. work handed over to 416th (EDINBURGH) Field Company R.E.	

Army Form C. 2118.

WAR DIARY
—or—
INTELLIGENCE SUMMARY.
(Erase heading not required.)

Instructions regarding War Diaries and Intelligence Summaries are contained in F.S. Regs., Part II. and the Staff Manual respectively. Title pages will be prepared in manuscript.

Place	Date	Hour	Summary of Events and Information	Remarks and references to Appendices
	21.9.18		II LIEUT. J.V.T. HENWOOD reports to C.R.E. for duty as assistant adjutant.	
	23rd		No 4. Section under LIEUT. J. ROBERTSON move to V.3.b.2.6. to prepare advanced Divisional H.Q's	
	24th		No 1. Section move to P.32.d.4.5. & report to 513 (LONDON) Field Company R.E. for duty. II LIEUT. A.R.LESLIE returns from 513 (LONDON) Field Coy R.E.	
	25th		Nos 2 & 3 Sections under MAJOR. J.T.F. HENDERSON. M.C. move to V.2.a.3.7. into Dugouts & Bivouacs	
	26th		CAPT. J.A. MERCER & Nos 1 & 4 Sections join forward H.Q'rs V.2.a.3.7. 2. OR's Reinforcements arrive from R.E. Base Depot.	
	27th		CAPT. J.A. MERCER & 4 Sections Sappers under MAJOR. J.T.F. HENDERSON. M.C. moved forward and established H.Q'rs at W.B.d.1.4. II LIEUT. A.R. LESLIE went forward to take charge of bridging vehicles & stores.	
		9.55.A.M.	4 Sections Sappers under LIEUT. J. ROBERTSON & LIEUT V.L. FARFAN moved forward to construct Infantry Bridges over CANAL DU NORD at W.15.a.9.8, and over AGACHE RIVER at W.15.b.7.7. On reaching the site it was discovered that the enemy still held the Eastern bank of Canal and fighting took place.	
		11.0 A.M.	1 Company 1/5th Khashire Rowers reported to MAJOR J.T.F. HENDERSON. M.C. for duty. 2 Lewis Gun teams of 1/5 Khashire Rowers went forward to reinforce Sappers.	
		11.15 A.M.	Bridging Stores went forward and were offloaded 400 yards West of Canal.	
		12.0 Noon	By 12.0 Noon the enemy was pushed back & work commenced on bridging the Canal. This was completed by 12.55. P.M. and route flagged as far as AGACHE RIVER	
		1.45 P.M.	By 1.45. P.M. crossing over AGACHE RIVER completed and Infantry across.	

Army Form C. 2118.

WAR DIARY
of
INTELLIGENCE SUMMARY.
(Erase heading not required.)

Instructions regarding War Diaries and Intelligence Summaries are contained in F. S. Regs., Part II. and the Staff Manual respectively. Title pages will be prepared in manuscript.

Place	Date	Hour	Summary of Events and Information	Remarks and references to Appendices
	27.9.18	3.0 P.M.	Reconnaissance was made of R.E. stores in captured area.	
		6.6.0 P.M.	Company H.Q.rs and Sappers moved to W.16.a.5.8.	
	30.	6.0 P.M.	Recd H.Q.rs & Transport moved to W.13.d.7.9, arriving at 7.0 P.M.	
			During the month the Company was employed as follows:- Constructing bridges over COJEUL RIVER & SENSEE RIVER, Erecting huts for Divisional H.Q.rs, repairs at Brigade H.Q.rs, Strengthening Dressing Station, repair and maintenance of forward roads, erection of Pontoon VIS-EN-ARTOIS, Strengthening cellars for advanced Dressing Bridge over canal at Q.22.d.6.2, Strengthening cellars for advanced Dressing Station at MARQUION, repairing bridge at Q.29.c.4.2, & clearing site and making road diversion for second bridge at slues point.	
			(All Map References on sheets 51B.S.W. Edition 3d (Local) & 51B S.E. Edition 5A (Local)).	

J. J. Abraham MAJOR R. E.
O/C 512th (LONDON) FIELD COY. R.

WAR DIARY or INTELLIGENCE SUMMARY

Army Form C. 2118.

512th (London) Field Coy R.E.

No. 33

C.R.E. 56th Division. Date 6/11/16

Place	Date	Hour	Summary of Events and Information	Remarks and references to Appendices
MARŒUIL	5.10.16		Lt. J. ROBERTSON proceeds on leave to UK	
"	9.		4 Sections Sappers under MAJOR. J.T.F. HENDERSON. M.C. mov by road to RUMAUCOURT into billets (farm)	
			Lt. DE CLERK proceeds to take over 2nd in command of 86th Field Coy R.E.	
			Lt. F.A. GREAVES joins for duty from 86th Field Coy R.E.	
			No. 346579 Corpl. E.C. CROSSLEY awarded the "MILITARY MEDAL"	
			No. 542253 A/Cpl. J. SAUNDERS awarded the "MILITARY MEDAL"	
"	13.		4 En. w MAJOR. J.T.F. HENDERSON M.C. & 3 sections Sappers moved forward to Sunken Road, R.26.a and stood by to construct Pontoon Bridges over Canal at ABB du VERGER Farm and AUBENCHEUL. 4 to 6 and sections under MAJOR. J.T.F. HENDERSON M.C. moved from R.26.a to ARLEUX to assist Infantry across Canal East of ARLEUX. Lt. G. saw No. 3 section returned to HQ RUMAUCOURT.	
"	15.		HQ transport under CAPT. T.A. MERCER mov by road to MARŒUIL into billets, first arriving 20.10	
"	16.		Remainder of Company under MAJOR. J.T.F. HENDERSON. M.C. mov by train to AGNEZ LES DUISANS, then by road to MARŒUIL arriving 23.15 into billets	
			Lt. A.R. LESLIE proceed on leave to UK.	
"	18.		52 re-enforcements arrive from R.E. Base	
			7.2. A.E. MK fired Company from R.E. Base Reinforcement	
"	20.		Company training	
"	31.		4 Sections under MAJOR. J.T.F. HENDERSON M.C. mov by bus to NOVELLES VERMELLES	

Army Form C. 2118.

WAR DIARY
or
INTELLIGENCE SUMMARY.
(Erase heading not required.)

512th (London) Field Coy R.E.

Instructions regarding War Diaries and Intelligence Summaries are contained in F.S. Regs., Part II. and the Staff Manual respectively. Title pages will be prepared in manuscript.

Place	Date	Hour	Summary of Events and Information	Remarks and references to Appendices

Arriving B+45 into Billets. Transport & HQ under CAPT. T.A. MERCER moved MARQUION by road arriving 19.30 into Billets pinpoint Y on K.14.11.15 from the remainder of Company at NOYELLES.

Company employed on:-
Erecting Heavy bridge over canal at Q29.C.4.0.
Reconstructing cells in forward areas.
Erecting shelters for Bakery. Erecting Brigade H.Q. Repairing huts.
At Ruyaulcourt in ruins. Strengthening & reconstructing Footbridges at Q.29.a.4.6. Q.23.d.9.5. Q.24.h.4.3. Recording Water levels.
Maintenance of bridges. Erecting trestle bridge at Q.23.a.4.0.35.
Erecting Hut for Divisional H.R.
Company training 19.30.
During Operations Company sustained Casualties 2 killed & 1 wounded.
All map references are on Sheet 57 S.E. 1:20,000.

H.B. Haddon
MAJOR R.E.
O/C 512th (LONDON) FIELD COY. R.E.

Army Form C. 2118.

WAR DIARY
or
INTELLIGENCE SUMMARY

Army Form C. 2118.

572 (London) Field Coy. R.E.

58th DIVISION 2/2/18

Place	Date	Hour	Summary of Events and Information	Remarks and references to Appendices
	27.10.18		Lieut. J. ROBERTSON awarded the MILITARY CROSS for gallantry in the field.	
	1.11.18		Lieut. F.A. GREAVES proceeds on leave to the U.K.	
NEUVELLES	2		Company move by road to THIANT arriving 15.00 hours into Billets.	
THIANT	4		Lieut. V.L. FARFAN and 4 O.R's attached to the Australian Light Horse & New Zealand Mounted Rifles as forward reconnaissance officer.	
			Company move by road to SAULTAIN arriving mid-day into Billets.	
SAULTAIN	5		Company move by road to SEBOURQUIAUX arriving 13.00 into Billets.	
SEBOURQUIAUX	6		Lieut. A.R. LESLIE returns from leave in U.K.	
	8		Company move by road to FOE DE SEIGNEUR arriving 6 o'clock into Billets.	
Fdse DE SEIGNEUR	9		Headquarters, No 2 Section & transport move to AUTREPPE arriving 10 o'clock & No 1 Section move to RUINSETTE arriving 8 o'clock. Lieut. J. ROBERTSON M.C. & No 1 Section attached to 168th Infantry Brigade for operations.	
RUINSETTE	10		No 3 & 4 Sections join their Company & Company move by road to LES COMMUNES arriving 14.15 into Billets.	
LESCOMMUNES	12		2 O.R's reinforcements arrive from R.E. Base Depot.	
	13		Lieut. J. ROBERTSON. M.C. & No 1 Section rejoin the Company.	
			Lieut. V.L. FARFAN & party rejoin the Company.	
	20		Lieut. F. GREAVES rejoins from leave in U.K.	

Army Form C. 2118.

WAR DIARY
or
INTELLIGENCE SUMMARY.

512ᵗʰ (London) Field Co R.E.

(Erase heading not required.)

Instructions regarding War Diaries and Intelligence Summaries are contained in F. S. Regs., Part II. and the Staff Manual respectively. Title pages will be prepared in manuscript.

Place	Date	Hour	Summary of Events and Information	Remarks and references to Appendices
	27.10.18		Company move by road to VILLERS ORS NICOLE arriving at 20 hours into billets.	
	"	10-0 R²	1 reinforcement arrived from R.E. Base Depot. Period 1-14. Company employed on Heavy Bridging, Trestle Bridging, Road maintenance, Searching for Booby Traps.	
		18-30	Training of Area improvement.	

H. Henderson Major R.E.
O/C 512ᵗʰ (LONDON) FIELD COY. R.E.

Army Form C. 2118.

WAR DIARY
INTELLIGENCE SUMMARY.
(Erase heading not required.)

512th (London) Field Coy R.E.

Vol 3 Dec 18

Place	Date	Hour	Summary of Events and Information	Remarks and references to Appendices
VILLERS	3.12.18		№546513 Sergt BENNETT. F. awarded the MILITARY MEDAL	
SIRE	4		Lt N.L. FARFAN rejoined from leave in UK.	
NOELE	7		MAJOR J.T.F. HENDERSON. M.C. proceeds on leave to the U.K. & CAPT. J. A MERCER	
	31		assumes command of the Company.	
			4 O.R. reinforcements arrive from R.E. Base Depot.	

J Mercer
CAPTAIN R.E.
o/c 512th (LONDON) FIELD COY. R.E.

Army Form C. 2118.

WAR DIARY
or
INTELLIGENCE SUMMARY.
(Erase heading not required.)

512th (London) Field Co. R.E.

WD 36

Place	Date	Hour	Summary of Events and Information	Remarks and references to Appendices
VILLERS	4.1.19		2 OR's reinforcement joined from R.E. Base Depot.	
SIRE	9		1 OR reinforcement joined from R.E. Base Depot.	
NICOLE	11		MAJOR. J.T.F. HENDERSON. M.C. returned from leave in UK. and resumed command of the Company.	
	13		1 OR reinforcement joined from R.E. Base Depot	
	16		2/Lt A.R. LESLIE proceed on leave to Paris.	
	23		CAPT. J.A. MERCER proceed on leave to U.K.	
	26		2/Lt A.E. DIX attached to CRE 56th Division for duty.	
	28		2/Lt A.R. LESLIE returned from leave in Paris.	

[signature]
O/C 512th (LONDON) FIELD COY. R.E.
MAJOR R.E.

512TH
(LONDON) FIELD COY.
R.E.
Date 1.2.1919.

Army Form C. 2118.

WAR DIARY
or
INTELLIGENCE SUMMARY.
(Erase heading not required.)

512th (London) Field Coy. R.E.

Vol 37

Place	Date	Hour	Summary of Events and Information	Remarks and references to Appendices
VILLERS SIRE NICOLE S.	1.2.19		2nd Lt. A.E. DIX leaves for demobilization.	JR
"	9. "		2nd Lt. F.A. GREAVES qualifies for rank of Lieutenant and wears badges of that rank.	JR
"	11. "		2nd Lt. A.R. LESLIE leaves for demobilization	JR
"	"		MAJOR. J.T.F. HENDERSON. M.C. hands over command of the Company to Lt. J. ROBERTSON. M.C.	JR
"	15. "		MAJOR. J.T.F. HENDERSON. M.C. leaves for demobilization.	JR
"	17 "		Company under Lt. J. ROBERTSON. M.C. move by road to QUESNES arriving 15.00 hours into Billets.	JR
QUESNES	18/28		NIL	

Robertson
CAPTAIN R.E.
O/C 512th (LONDON) FIELD COY. R.E.

Army Form C. 2118.

WAR DIARY
or
INTELLIGENCE SUMMARY.

(Erase heading not required.)

512th (LONDON) Field Coy R.E.

Army Form C. 2118.

Instructions regarding War Diaries and Intelligence Summaries are contained in F. S. Regs., Part II. and the Staff Manual respectively. Title pages will be prepared in manuscript.

512TH (LONDON) FIELD COY. R.E.

Place	Date	Hour	Summary of Events and Information	Remarks and references to Appendices
CUESMES	2/3/19		MAJOR J.A. MERCER rejoined from leave in the U.K. and resumed command of Company.	
" "	5/3/19		CAPTAIN J. ROBERTSON, M.C. proceeds on leave to the U.K.	
" "	24/2/19		LIEUT. F.A. GREAVES proceeds to join No. 20 Defense Sub Section for duty	
" "	29/2/19		CAPTAIN J. ROBERTSON, M.C. rejoined from leave in the U.K.	

[signature] MAJOR R.E.
O/C 512th (LONDON) FIELD COY. R.E.

Army Form C. 2118.

WAR DIARY
or
INTELLIGENCE SUMMARY.
(Erase heading not required.)

512 (London) Field Co. R.E.

Place	Date	Hour	Summary of Events and Information	Remarks and references to Appendices
OUESMES	3.4.19		CAPT. J. ROBERTSON. M.C. reports to C.R.E. 56th Division for duties as Acting Adjutant.	
"	4	10 am	moved to C.R.E. 9th Scotland Division. Transferred to service of occupation.	
"	5		Lt. V.L. FARFAN proceeds on special leave to COLOGNE.	
"	8		CAPT. J. ROBERTSON. M.C. transferred to H.Q. C.R.E. 56th Division as Adjutant.	
"	14		Lt. V.L. FARFAN rejoins from special leave.	
	15/30		– Nil –	

MAJOR R.E.
O.C. 512th (LONDON) FIELD COY. R.E.

2/1 London Fd Coy RE
56   Feb
    Vol I

www.ingramcontent.com/pod-product-compliance
Lightning Source LLC
Chambersburg PA
CBHW081437160426
43193CB00013B/2308